City Diplomacy

City Diplomacy
From City-States to Global Cities

Raffaele Marchetti

University of Michigan Press

Ann Arbor

For questions or permissions, please contact um.press.perms@umich.edu

Published in the United States of America by the
University of Michigan Press
Manufactured in the United States of America
Printed on acid-free paper
First published October 2021

A CIP catalog record for this book is available from the British Library.

Library of Congress Cataloging-in-Publication Data

Names: Marchetti, Raffaele, author.
Title: City diplomacy : from city-states to global cities / Raffaele Marchetti.
Description: Ann Arbor : University of Michigan Press, 2021. | Includes bibliographical
    references and index. |
Identifiers: LCCN 2021018738 (print) | LCCN 2021018739 (ebook) |
    ISBN 9780472075034 (hardcover) | ISBN 9780472055036 (paperback) |
    ISBN 9780472129454 (ebook)
Subjects: LCSH: Metropolitan areas—Political aspects. | Sociology, Urban. |
    Urban climatology.
Classification: LCC HT330 .M377   2021 (print) | LCC HT330 (ebook) |
    DDC 307.76—dc23
LC record available at https://lccn.loc.gov/2021018738
LC ebook record available at https://lccn.loc.gov/2021018739

Cover image courtesy Shutterstock.com / sdecoret

Contents

Digital materials related to this title can be found on the Fulcrum platform via the following citable URL: https://doi.org/10.3998/mpub.11991621

Acknowledgments

I wish to express sincere thanks to my Luiss students in the Department of Political Sciences and the School of Government: Hadeer Ibrahim Abdelmagid, Mattia Bonizzato, Giacomo Bozio Madè, Federica Castellana, Filippo Cutrera, Clara Houin, and Maria Vittoria Fiori, for having made available part of the material of their degree theses on different aspects of city diplomacy carried out under my supervision. With their discussions in class and their research they helped me to refine this book. Many thanks to Judit Fabian and Manfredi Valeriani for insightfully commenting on the text. I wish to thank Daniel Monti and Fredric Nachbaur for their encouragement regarding this book. I wish to thank Samson Fagbohunlu for proofreading the text. Last but not least, I want to express my gratitude to Elizabeth Demers from the University of Michigan Press for her enthusiastic support of this project.

Setting the Stage

The Relevance of Cities in Global Affairs

Cities are where the action is. We need to change our mental map—reality is changing fast and we are stuck to a state-centric understanding of international affairs. After being identified as the sites of action for many centuries, cities were kicked out of the mental scene with the Peace of Westphalia in 1648. Today, cities are getting more attention, but we often don't realize it fully because we continue to think in a predominantly Westphalian manner. Our mental map consists of approximately 200 pieces, the states that are members of the United Nations, but these are not the only pieces of the jigsaw puzzle we need to have in mind to capture the world in which we live. We need at least another 10,000 pieces in our minds, the rough number of cities in the world.[1]

Socioeconomic Relevance

In 2007, for the first time in history, more people lived in urban areas than in rural areas. The global population living in cities moved from 3 percent (1800), to 14 percent (1900), to 30 percent (1950), to 40 percent (2000), and is today 55 percent (World Bank 2019), with an estimated prospect of 70 percent by 2050. The prospect for the future includes some massive urban conglomerates that mankind has never experienced in its history. For instance, in 2015, Kinshasa, DRC, had a population of 12 million but is projected to reach 83 million by 2100; Lagos Metropolitan Area, Nigeria, is projected to reach the enormous population of 80 to 100 million by 2100 (Hoornweg and Pope 2014). Mexico City already has as many as 100,000 members in its police force, larger than the law enforcement agencies of 115 countries. Over the past fifty years the number of nation-states doubled to reach 193, but the number and size of cities with more than 100,000 people increased tenfold over the same period to over 4,000. Today there are 33 megacities (those typically with a population over 10 million people), and the number will continue to rise (United Nations 2019).

Today the most significant activities take place in cities, yet we "see" only states as the actors in the world. Economic growth and fiscal experiments take place in urban contexts. Cities are the center of the world economy, responsible for 80 percent of global GDP (World Bank 2019). Political reforms, social innovation, and protests and revolutions also occur in cities. Criminal activities, terrorist actions, counterinsurgencies, missile attacks (indeed atomic bombs), and wars are developed in cities. Pandemics spread in large urban conglomerates. Cities are sources of global pollution (80 percent of carbon emissions come from cities) as well as sites of environmental transformations such as urban gardening. Knowledge production, big data collection, and tech innovation are all spurred by intense urban interaction as well as social surveillance and crime prevention. Cities are the meeting points of cultures, religions, and identities. Cities are the pivots of civilizations and the cradle of the future.

Global cities are the pivotal center of the system that connects people around the planet. Cities influence globalization, but are also strongly influenced by it. New York City manages an annual budget of roughly $88 billion, bigger than the national budgets of 120 countries around the world. The economic output of metropolitan Seoul—home to half of the South Korean population—is larger than that of many nation-states. Some cities are already globalized, and many others are globalizing. From this perspective, cities are more important than states because all these phenomena tend to take place in cities. This new type of city has an inherent cosmopolitan nature. Global cities offer promising spaces to rethink politics, a counterweight to the rise of national populism and ethnic discrimination. In a sense, cities are the vanguard of the global cosmopolis, with people from everywhere—with different faiths, languages, and cultures—living and working close to each other. Cities are nodes of integration for melting pots or rather civic mosaics that accommodate and value pluralism. They are living experiments of rooted cosmopolitanism (Tarrow 2005).

The process of internationalization, and indeed of globalization, has brought both good and bad news for cities. They have not only new opportunities to play an international role and increase the welfare of their own citizens, but also present risks and threats that cross borders and more often than not produce impacts locally (pollution, natural disasters, terrorism, epidemics, violence, financial and economic shocks). With information and communication technologies removing barriers and reducing geographical distances, the level of connectivity has dramatically increased.

Being connected entails both risks and opportunities. Cities are increasingly learning to take advantage of the latter and avoid the former. It is now easier for municipalities to reach out to the international arena to enhance their world relevance. For instance, they can attract corporations, investors, and travelers and host global events. At the same time, as the COVID-19 crisis teaches us, cities remain highly vulnerable to global threats. Cities are the hotbeds of viruses. Wuhan, New York, Milan, Madrid, Paris, and London proved that urban agglomerations are perfect locations for spurring global pandemics.

Political Relevance

Global politics is shaped significantly by a number of cities that are increasingly active on the world stage. They develop twinning networks and projects, share information, sign cooperation agreements, contribute to the drafting of national and international policies, provide development aid, promote assistance to refugees, and do territorial marketing through decentralized city-city or district-district cooperation. Decentralization and subsidiarity play an import role in creating the political opportunities structure within which cities go international. Cities do what "municipalities" used to do many centuries ago: they cooperate, but also enter intense competitive dynamics. For this reason, we need to have at least two mental maps in mind, the state-centered map and the non-state-centered map, if we want to understand current sociopolitical dynamics on a planetary level. In particular, as regards diplomacy, we must take into account the existence of a complex diplomatic regime, one based on different levels that at times overlap with each other.

We tend to take the Peace of Westphalia in 1648 as the beginning of modern international diplomacy. And yet, the previous record of diplomacy was extremely rich, and it was carried out to a large extent by cities, from classic Greek cities and Athenian diplomacy to the experience of Renaissance Italy, with the diplomatic corps and missions abroad of Florence. Vast city-states such as Chengdu in China and Venice in Italy used to play an outsized role in shaping the terms of trade between societies. Then, in the seventeenth century, the new state-centered system marginalized the cities, which were absorbed into the nation-states. In recent years, however, cities are back (together with many other nonstate or substate actors). After a 300-year hiatus, cities are getting more involved in mediating global relations; to a certain extent, they are resuming functions they once performed. Today, as they did historically, cities are forming a new diplomatic corps—with mayors, urban planners, city entrepreneurs, local cultural leaders, academics, and "supercops" serving as emissaries. This is due in part to the irresistible pressures of urbanization.

City diplomacy expresses the willingness of citizens to have another point of access to world affairs. Both for traditional pivotal cities and for emerging municipalities, city diplomacy provides an opportunity to engage with foreign counterparts and possibly gain important benefits. By upgrading their organizational form, redirecting their resources, devising a sophisticated brand strategy, and leveraging their growing soft power, cities can persuade foreign actors of a different nature to cooperate in various policy domains. Cities engage with international institutions, foreign governments, nongovernmental organizations, business firms, and many other types of actors on the world scene. A significant component of such international projects is developed between the cities through multilateral networks, bilateral partnership, and joint initiatives.

We need to rethink the way we understand the scope of city activities. They are both inward and outward looking. They play a multilayered game in which local, national, and international strategies are highly integrated simply because they cannot be played out in isolation. Hence the importance of city networks and other multi-stakeholder initiatives. The international action of cities, which consists of different vectors beyond the classic economic one, presents many risks but also many opportunities. "Nations talk, cities act," as Michael Bloomberg, former mayor of New York City, famously stated, but there are also constraints in such actions. Going international is not easy: resources for international activities are limited, entering the circles of international affairs is not always easy, and the normative framework at times resists the inclusion of cities in global affairs. There is always the risk of remaining in the self-referential bubble of the "world of cities" and being unable to have a significant impact on the "real" world. And yet, cities proved skillful enough year after year to activate a virtuous circle of sustainable development and growing expertise that allowed them to achieve significant goals at the international level.

Cities act diplomatically by themselves, but also, increasingly, in partnership with national government and international organizations. Spotting the windows of opportunity that are available to cities at the international level, national governments are quickly learning to take advantage of urban attractiveness to indirectly pursue their national foreign policy goals; they use cities as proxies, which sometimes generates international political controversies. On the opposite, however, cities can sometimes take an international direction that is in stark contrast to that of their national government, which can generate national controversies. Beyond government, international organizations and business corporations have also recognized the value of cities and boosted cooperation with them. The UN has increasingly acknowledged the contributions of local authorities in addressing transnational challenges and shaping global governance. In the field of sustainable development, for instance, the United Nations and its agencies have been seeking the active involvement of municipalities, thanks to their capability to implement on the ground objectives agreed to at a global level. Recently, cities have been invited to preparatory meetings and high-level talks within the following UN-led processes: the Sendai Framework for Disaster Risk Reduction (June 2015), the adoption of the Sustainable Development Goals by the UN General Assembly (September 2015), the Paris Agreement on Climate Change (December 2015), and the Conference on Housing and Sustainable Urban Development (UN Habitat, October 2016), among others.

In such a favorable and cooperative framework, cities and other subnational governments are pressing to achieve formal recognition on the world stage not just as mere observers but as full-fledged actors. Therefore, they are now advocating for a special status in the UN General Assembly that would allow them to take part in defining policies with territorial impact. The European Union includes cities and local authorities within the activities of the Committee of Regions. This mainly consists of tailor-made projects of cross-border cooperation among cities, based on local dialogue and bottom-up approaches through which financial resources are allocated efficiently and in line with matching requests and offers. Corporations and private foundations have also started to work with cities. The Rockefeller Foundation's past initiative 100 Resilient Cities, created in 2013, aimed at supporting cities around the world to become more resilient in response to the increasing physical, social, and economic challenges of the twenty-first century. It relied on important partners from the private, public, academic, and nonprofit sectors, including Microsoft, Ernst & Young, the International Rescue Committee, Save the Children, Siemens, and the World Wildlife Fund. As always, the external funding from international institutions or private companies constitutes an opportunity, but also an exogenous element of agenda setting for the internationalization of cities.

City diplomacy is experiencing a resurgence for several reasons. Internally, local politicians see clear political opportunities for visibility and electoral gains. But city diplomacy can also derive from the rising pressure of citizens' activism from below, as in the case of denuclearized municipalities. City diplomacy can also serve as a functional substitute for national diplomacy, in two directions—cities to foreign entities or foreign entities to cities. In the former case, cities may be part of territories that claim sovereignty but still lack official international recognition, as in Palestinian cities for Palestine and Barcelona for Catalonia, both of which actively seek international engagement. In the latter case, we find those territories that, lacking bilateral accreditation, seek an alternative way to get recognition by engaging with foreign local authorities, as in the case of Abkhazia and South Ossetia. Finally, para-diplomacy could simply be a tool to better serve the interests of the city: Amsterdam, for example, is active in Ghana, Suriname, and Turkey because these are countries of origin of its immigrants. Similarly, cities engage in conflict resolution in other countries to prevent migratory inflows. There are also external reasons for the boom in para-diplomacy. Global politics is increasingly marked by the presence of intrusive transnational networks that push cities to react for both global and local reasons. In the same way, local authorities at times go international because they are invited to participate in global affairs by international organizations; a typical case is the strong push the EU gives for the engagement in Brussels-based European affairs by the cities of the different EU member states. Finally, certain socioeconomic and institutional conditions make city diplomacy more likely. The adoption by citizens and political elites of an "internationalist" political culture, the availability of material resources (money, human resources, etc.), the geographical proximity to borders or hubs (such as large ports), and relative autonomy from central government or, alternatively, sufficient representation of local interests in central government to promote alliances between the two levels, are all factors that increase the likelihood of a vital city diplomacy.

Beyond the instrumental dimension, international city activism ultimately has a normative value. Cities are now the level of government that more directly affects the majority of the world's population, and thus they should have a stake in influencing certain global policies. They have a closer relation with their citizens than nation-states, and city-level decisions definitely influence people's daily lives much more concretely. In addition, when poor policies are carried out by central governments, it is likely that urban areas will suffer the worst effects. When the state is unable to serve the interests and support the rights of citizens, or does so inefficiently, cities are called on to complement or replace the state. This has an obvious compensatory value as a functional substitute for state deficiencies. Indeed, Barber and a number of mayors have claimed that cities have the right and duty to respond to the dysfunctionality of states; they have the right to govern themselves in the true spirit of self-determination and perhaps of democracy itself (B. Barber 2013). From this point of view, democratic principle requires cities' international activism to give citizens a real possibility to determine their fate by shaping the norms that govern public life. Cities become normative mediators between the world and the state. This function of cities is crucial because of their special characteristics as democratically organized communities in which place is not only imagined, but lived (Blank 2006).

Scholarly Relevance and the Aim of This Book

In the academic debate, after being marginalized for a long time, attention to the international dimension of cities is growing (Acuto 2010, 2013a, 2013b; Acuto, Morissette, and Tsouros 2017; B. Barber 2013; Chan 2016; Curtis 2014; Gutierrez-Camps 2013; Hocking 1993; Hocking, Melissen, Riordan, and Sharp 2012; Leffel 2018; Terruso 2016; Tuirán Sarmiento 2016; Van Der Pluijm and Melissen 2007; Viltard 2010). The fields of geography and urban studies have had an obvious interest in the topic, but they typically considered the international dimension to be of secondary importance. Economists have looked more at the inside-outside dynamics of cities in the global economy, but their interest in the governance dimension is limited. Political studies and International Relations (IR) were supposed to be the disciplines better equipped to capture these diplomatic dimensions, yet they struggled to focus on cities as independent international actors. Today, most IR scholars would resist considering cities as relevant international actors. Cities are sometimes considered as sites *for* IR, not *of* IR, or simply as lower-level administrative units. They are not typically assigned full international political agency, with few exceptions. Acuto and Curtis have provided first significant advances in terms of capturing the international agency of cities (Acuto 2013a; Curtis 2014). What is missing is a full characterization of their features, including their functioning as actors, their strategies, and their repertoire of actions and fields of operation; the intent of this book is to provide such a characterization.

With this book, I aim to enrich the scholarship on complex pluralism (Cerny 2010; Ferguson 2015; Ferguson and Mansbach 2008; Marchetti 2016; McFarland 2004) by focusing on the role of cities in global affairs. To help construct a subfield out of existing fragments of literature from IR and global city studies, I highlight the insights produced by linking city diplomacy to IR, i.e., the role of city diplomacy in both facilitating and undermining IR. Complex pluralism assumes a conception of politics as managed by many different actors, be they state or nonstate actors (NSAs), who interact, coalesce, cooperate, and compete among themselves, alone or in synergy, to have a political impact on multiple institutional layers below, above, inside, and across states. The results of such moves impinge significantly on the socioeconomic dynamics that shape our lives. It is pluralist because there are different kinds of actors with different levels of power, alternative normative values, and divergent political projects. And it is complex because these actors interact with each other in sophisticated ways for both peaceful and violent purposes. The pluralization of actors in the international or indeed global domain not only generates complexity, it changes the nature of the system itself. Its ontology, dynamics, ordering principles, and outcomes heavily depend on these multiple interactions. Power is distributed and a certain degree of institutional cooperation is in place, yet the international system populated by states, international organizations (IOs), multinational corporations (MNCs), nongovernmental organizations (NGOs), and other such groups remains fluid and ultimately anarchic (Prichard 2017). Globalization has changed the institutional matrix of power in IR: the old focus on institutional politics at the national and supranational levels, and state actors as political agents, has given way to a multilevel array of actors, institutions, and practices. Compared to the last few centuries of international affairs, the new political agency of nongovernmental actors can indeed be seen as revolutionary in terms of both changes and challenges. This plethora of actors act strategically within intermingled political-opportunity structures. They try to take advantage of the openings provided by the interstices of international politics and to avoid the constraints that more powerful actors impose on them. Cities are a very significant class of nonstate actors in global politics, yet they remain largely marginal to the scholarly debate. This book aims to study the overall trends and best practices of city diplomacy to enrich our understanding of the global politics in which we all live.

In 1795 Immanuel Kant wrote the famous pamphlet, *Zum Ewingen Frieden* (Perpetual Peace) (Kant 1795; reprinted 1991). It was considered a pathbreaking work because it broadened the conception of political realms that had dominated the intellectual reflection for centuries. Kant suggested focusing on three distinct levels of social interaction to implement the principles that would lead to perpetual peace in a self-executing manner. The first principle focuses on the domestic level: "*The Civil Constitution in every State shall be Republican.*" The second principle looks at the intergovernmental level: "*The Right of Nations shall be founded on a Federation of Free States.*" The third principle points to the global dimension: "*The Rights of men as Citizens of the world in a cosmo-political system, shall be restricted to conditions of universal Hospitality."* While Kant was clearly innovative, he didn't acknowledge the city level. From the vantage point of today, we need to consider adding a fourth principle with reference to the local level: *"Urban Communities shall be cogoverned by their citizens and open to the world."* Together with the individual, national, and international levels, we need to reckon with the city level. Somehow similarly, in 1988 Robert Putnam wrote a famous article on the logic of two-level games (Putnam 1988). He suggested that politicians need to balance their action between the domestic and the international domains to be effective. After thirty years, we need to update Putnam's intuition pointing to a three-level or indeed multilevel game: local, national, and global at the same time. Today, in thinking about a comprehensive and effective restructuring of the political system that aims at stability, development, and democracy, we can no longer omit the city level.

Part I • Cities in Global Affairs

Our traditional mental map of international politics tends to see the globe as a jigsaw puzzle composed of approximately 200 tiles: the 193 states that are official members of the United Nations. From this viewpoint, to understand international politics, we have to observe the behavior of states, which we take to be the units of analysis of the international system. This state-centric world view derives from the experience of the Westphalian system and the intellectual dominance of Realism. Throughout history, however, the nature of the international system has not always been perceived like this.

Before the Westphalian system, the world was read as divided between large (supranational) empires, and history as the product of their interaction. During the Cold War, the mental map of international politics was based essentially only on two tiles, the two blocks, capitalist and socialist, with Washington and Moscow as capitals, with the third world of nonaligned countries in a truly marginal position. From the late 1970s until the 2008 financial crisis, according to many commentators the global jigsaw had 5 or 8 pieces, the member states of the G5 and G8. The North of the world, the West, guided the world no longer by colonial control but through economic leadership. Since the 1990s, however, Huntington has argued that the real jigsaw of world politics is not made up of 194, or 2, or 8, or 20 pieces, but by 9 macro pieces that he calls civilizations (Huntington 1993, 1996). According to this American scholar, history today is decided by the interaction of 9 macroregional areas: (1) Western, which includes North America (without Mexico), Western Europe, the Philippines, Australia, New Zealand, and Papua New Guinea; (2) Orthodox, which runs from Greece to Russia, taking in Kazakhstan and Bosnia-Herzegovina; (3) Islamic, stretching from Morocco to Indonesia, passing through Albania, from Sunnis to Shiites, but without a lead country; (4) African, including only the sub-Saharan countries; (5) Latin American, from Argentina to Mexico; (6) Hindu, centered on India; (7) Sinic, centered on China, excluding Tibet but including Vietnam and the entire Korean Peninsula; (8) Buddhist, with Tibet, Mongolia, and other countries in Southeast Asia; and finally, (9) Japan, on its own. More recently we came to realize that the G8 states were no longer able to govern the world alone and as a consequence the map was widened to a number of countries in the South of the world, the so-called emerging powers. The meetings of the G20 would institutionalize this geostrategic enlargement. In sum, then, throughout history mental maps of international affairs have changed more or less rapidly.

The mental maps presented above are linked to a number of models for the international system which suggests different distributions of power. A classic model (in the terms of the last twenty years at least) is that of America's unipolarism, in which the world continues to be led by the USA because it is the unchallengeable military, economic, and political power. This kind of interpretation represents a traditional and widely held view across the US government. According to this perspective, the USA is destined to guide the rest of the world, given its exceptional nature, the "shining city upon a hill," which gives it a role of responsibility toward the rest of the international community. We find this vision embedded in both the Republicans' (Bush 2002) and the Democrats' (Obama 2007) reading of US world leadership, but also among many scholars (Kagan 1998; Krauthammer 2003) and in many official documents (Department of Defense 2012).

A second much-discussed model is the so-called G2 between the USA and China, whereby the two superpowers of our age confront each other in an atmosphere of increasing rivalry and the destiny of the international community is seen to depend on the resolution of this competition. According to the most accredited data, in aggregate terms the Chinese economy is destined to become the largest in the world, having surpassed the Japanese economy in 2010. The USA, after a long period of world economic primacy, is thus doomed to relinquish the top position in favor of China's (re)emerging power, which accounts for around 20 percent of global GDP, the position it had before European colonial expansion. In IR debates, the prediction about the outcome of the Sino-American competition remains very controversial. According to some American liberals, the change in economic leadership will not destabilize the international system because existing international institutions may prove sufficiently robust to handle the change while forcing the new leader to accept the current rules (Ikenberry 2011). Other American realists, however, expect the United States to continue to be the hegemon, but also submit that were it to decline, the international system as we know it would change radically insofar as it is the byproduct of power distribution (Kagan 2012). In the very recent years with the Trump and Xi leaderships, the tension between the two countries increased significantly, pushing the international system toward a new phase of polarization. From the perspective of the G2, much will depend on the kind of relationship that will be established between the USA and China, i.e. cooperative, win-win, or competitive, zero sum.

A third model is a tripolar system led by the USA, the EU, and China. According to this perspective, the logic of the old triad of the USA, the EU, and Japan would see China take the Asian role, but the system would remain substantially unaltered with most of the world's economic, military, and political interactions taking place among the three macroregions that have imperialistic features (Khanna 2008). The change would, however, be in the different political perspective that would animate the regions involved. While Japan has been aligned with the political vision of the Western world, today's scenario is unprecedented.

A fourth, much-discussed model is that of a multipolar world in which, alongside the USA and the EU, emerging countries consolidate their position, especially Brazil, Russia, India, and China, with the addition of South Africa. But other countries also have considerable economic weight, such as Mexico, Indonesia, Turkey, South Korea, and Australia. According to this perspective, the world is thus moving toward a roughly balanced, if unprecedented, model of power, because for the first time after many centuries the Western countries must share power with other countries from the South of the world.

Beyond these significant four state-centered models, there is another one that is arguably important to capture the complexity of the world today. It is a model we need to take into account if we want to understand contemporary city diplomacy. This fifth model is of a nonpolar world (Avant, Finnemore, and Sell 2010; Haass 2008; Hale and Held 2011; Khanna 2011)—a world in which power is spread across many players, including nongovernmental actors. This is a world strongly molded by globalization, and the model rejects realist state-centric exclusivity. From this viewpoint, the best conceptual map to guide our understanding and actions in the global age is much more complex than the previous maps we examined. On the one side, the state as a unitary actor is seeing its central role wane in favor of disaggregation into substate authorities with increasing transnational agency (Slaughter 2003, 2004). Transnational governing networks are acquiring ever more importance: courts, public authorities, interparliamentary assemblies, and central banks are all increasing their cooperation with international counterparts. Local authorities such as cities and regions are following precisely the same pattern. On the other side, the number and range of nongovernmental actors, both for-profit and not-for-profit, is increasing, and they demand inclusion in the international decision-making process or directly acquire authority, expertise, and power to influence international affairs in parallel to and regardless of state authority. Nonstate actors are everywhere in global politics (Khanna 2011; Naìm 2013), including such groups as the World Economic Forum; global terrorism groups such as Al-Qaeda or Daesh; philanthropic foundations such as the Bill & Melinda Gates Foundation; social movements such as Movimento Sem Terra; international NGOs such as Greenpeace and Amnesty International; the Tibetan diaspora; alternative media such as Wikileaks; the stars of charitable work such as Bono of U2; think tanks such as the Council on Foreign Relations; banks such as JP Morgan Chase; rating agencies such as Standard and Poor; and major global media players such as CNN or the new media such as Facebook and Twitter. Cities and regions are among the most innovative nonstate actors today.

Politics in the era of globalization is much more complex than in previous eras. Phenomena in one location are often connected with phenomena in others locations. To have political control of a dynamic that develops on multiple dimensions, levels, and locations requires advanced skills in understanding, judgment, and innovation. Unlike in the past, today, American mortgages are directly connected to the well-being of Icelanders, the prime minister of Iceland can be forced to resign after an angry employee of a Panamanian law firm leaks information on a fiscal safe haven, health infrastructure in Indonesia influences flu deaths in Mexico, and the rate of car ownership in China is central for the survival of the inhabitants of the Tuvalu islands. In such an intertwined world, governance cannot function effectively if it is restricted to governments only. There is an ample recognition that to enhance legitimacy and improve effectiveness, global governance needs to include NSAs as well. These functional reasons are among the key drivers for the consolidation of city diplomacy in world affairs that took place in the last few decades.

1 • Nonstate Actors in Global Politics

Global Governance and the Pluralization of International Affairs

The current institutional frame is composed of different elements, including state, intergovernmental, and transnational organizations. The international correlate of domestic state institutions is conventionally known as the state system. Arising almost simultaneously with the state itself, the state system was grounded on the institution of classical sovereignty and international law, which was rarely a stable system. A distinct break was marked in the middle of the twentieth century with the establishment of the United Nations, a remedial institution constructed on an inherently deficient juxtaposition of classic, liberal, and cosmopolitan elements (Held 2002; Held and McGrew 2002). In recent decades a strengthening of multilateral political engagement has paralleled and at times challenged the United Nations' order, creating a new system of global governance. The mushrooming of intergovernmental (e.g., the G7/8 meetings) and (semi) private agencies (e.g., the Internet Corporation for Assigned Names and Numbers [ICANN], or the Society for Worldwide Interbank Financial Telecommunication [SWIFT]) has put under pressure, if not supplanted, the traditional UN-centered international system, creating alternative mechanisms of global governance (Avant et al. 2010; Hale and Held 2011).

In the last few decades the international institutional framework has changed significantly with the substantial increase and intensification of the mechanisms of global governance (Czempiel and Rosenau 1992; Hale and Held 2011; Koenig-Archibugi and Zürn 2006; Risse 2011; Rosenau 1997; Weiss and Wilkinson 2019; Zürn 2018). The model of embedded liberalism—a combination of free-market and national-welfare policies (Ruggie 1982)—has increased the need for wider and deeper international cooperation, which has finally led to the establishment of a dense network of hybrid and monofunctional organizations (Slaughter 2004; Zürn 2004). Constant growth of political norms and legal dispositions, with a low level of democracy, has become increasingly characteristic of the institutional side of present-day society, eroding the legitimacy of both the state and classic international law. It is within this new system of global governance that local authorities managed to increase the room for maneuvering at the international level.

Global governance is distinguished from classic government because it does not require the same level of centralization, formalization, and integration. Global governance is based on norms, rules, and procedures designed to solve problems at a global level, but does not require a unique source of power. Among the characteristics of the current system of global governance, the following are the most important. First, every form of governance covers an ample spectrum of actors, given that it directly regards a system of multilateral rules at a global, transnational, national, or regional level (Held and McGrew 2002, 8–13). The rules of governance tend to be much more intrusive compared to traditional intergovernmental rules, and generate demands for increased legitimacy (Woods 2000, 217). Second, notwithstanding its wider spectrum, the system of governance is more limited in terms of focus, since it concerns only specific issues and the agents involved therein (stakeholders) (Krasner 1982, 185), but at the same time it is more inclusive in that it goes beyond the state-only rule of participation. Third, by being multilateral (including three or more actors), it induces generalized principles of behavior and wide reciprocity (Caporaso 1993; Keohane 1986; Ruggie 1993). Moreover, governance is polyarchic, given that it includes different authorities such as states, subnational groups, and special transnational interests, often on a formally unequal stage (Rosenau 1992, 284–85). Global governance thus implies a change in the concept of international agency, insofar as states and the United Nations become increasingly integrated with a number of other structures of multilateral governance.

Rosenau and Czmpiel perceive global governance as a totality of regulatory mechanisms not emanating from an official authority, but generated by the proliferation of networks in an increasingly interdependent world (Czempiel and Rosenau 1992). Global governance is seen not as a result but as a continuous process that is never fixed and has no single model or form (Koenig-Archibugi and Zürn 2006). Regulation is not simply a body of established rules, it is also the ongoing result of a permanent game of interactions, conflicts, compromises, negotiations, and reciprocal adjustments.

Five tendencies characterize the recent forms of global governance: (1)

the fusion of the national and the international, (2) the increased role of nonstate players, (3) the emergence of private governance, (4) the move to a new method of compliance, and (5) the growing complexity of the institutional horizon (Avant et al. 2010; Hale and Held 2011). It is necessary to analyze these tendencies one by one.

First, national politics are increasingly influenced by international politics, but the latter, too, remains strongly dependent on national political dynamics, in a reciprocal link that seems difficult to resolve. The neologism "inter-mestic," combining international and domestic, is often applied to such circumstances. Already in the 1970s Keohane and Nye had begun to study the phenomenon of interdependence (Nye and Keohane 1971). In the 1980s Putnam's famous study marked a milestone in the debate about constantly balancing the two dimensions (Putnam 1988). More recently Slaughter pointed to the importance of transnational networks (Slaughter 2004).

Second, nonstate actors (NSAs) have increasingly become protagonists at the international level. By the 1970s their relevance had already been a subject of study (Keohane and Nye 1977, 1971). In the 1980s it was relatively marginalized because of the revival of neoliberal institutionalism. In the 1990s NSAs were again the subject of important studies (Keck and Sikkink 1998; Risse-Kappen 1995), but they remained subordinated to interactions among states. It is only in the last decade that it has become evident that NSAs can influence global politics in an autonomous way.

Third, global governance is increasingly private (Hall and Biersteker 2002). While traditional authority at the international level relied on the principle of delegation and was embedded in an institutional form, today we increasingly witness the consolidation of new forms of authority that are far more privatistic. Authority is thus recognized in private subjects not on the basis of delegation through mostly electoral mechanisms, but on the basis of expertise (as, for example, when technocrats gain power in decision-making processes) (Fisher 1990), or the basis of moral credibility (consider, for instance, the prestige enjoyed by NGOs or celebrities) (Busby 2007; Kapoor 2012), or the basis of the ability to accomplish a specific duty (take, for example, the mercenaries contracted to wage armed conflicts, or the NGOs working on cooperation and development) (Hulme and Edwards 1997).

Fourth, respect for rules is obtained through soft authority rather than coercive power. Traditionally, respect for rules was obtained through formal sanctions. Today, however, rules are not necessarily formal, and their enforcement does not necessarily involve sanctions. What are used, rather, are voluntary regulations, recommendations, best practices, transparency, and accountability. There is a shift from the "command and control" model to a "managerial approach," which is substantiated by the improvement in the ability and the will of the actors to comply with international standards through actions of capacity-building and normative persuasion (Avant et al. 2010). This shift is in some way made necessary by the lack of a single central authority empowered to sanction, and also by the simultaneous functional need to respect shared standards. These standards (1) can thus be created by very different actors, (2) can apply as a whole to a group of highly diversified actors that require nonrestrictive rules to obtain consensus more easily, (3) imply low costs for their formulation, and (4) are complied with as a result of the important role played by persuasion.

Fifth, the institutional panorama is increasingly complex. The proliferation of international institutions, whether intergovernmental, hybrid, or private, transforms how politics is conducted and the strategies adopted by actors in global politics. This can be seen, for instance, in the consolidation of (even hybrid) institutions composed only of like-minded actors. Increasingly frequent is the phenomenon of the so-called shopping forum, in which the actors search for the most favorable institutional and juridical framework.

The concept of global governance can be seen as the expression of a gradual departure from the classic Westphalian system (decentralized, with its emphasis on the rights of sovereignty and political independence, and on the principle of nonintervention) toward a less conflictual, more cooperative and consensual system. Apart from the different interpretations of global governance, an important normative question concerns the problem of the legitimacy of these global institutions regarding the issue of exclusion (Marchetti 2008). The world's growing interdependence increases the need to have institutions capable of regulating interaction among the different international players, fostering cooperation that could not be achieved through the uncoordinated calculations of interest in a heterogeneous sphere of political action. In this sense, global governance depends on the level of efficiency in addressing issues, which is linked to the amplified participation of governmental and nongovernmental actors alike. The rise of cities in global affairs stems from this nexus of effectiveness and legitimacy.

The dynamics of globalization have accentuated the diminishing exclusivity of the states as actors in international relations. Globalization ties distant communities together, deterritorializing relations of power and extending their reach beyond traditional national borders. Diminishing the exclusivity of states as international actors, globalization has opened up space for new social players. Beyond the states and intergovernmental organizations that have occupied a central place in international life since their origin (think of the United Nations), the system of global governance is currently populated by a variety of other international and transnational actors that have a strong say on international affairs. To understand today's global politics we cannot limit ourselves to observing state or intergovernmental action; we should also consider the actions of other NSAs. Among these, four types are particularly relevant: profit-oriented transnational enterprises; the nongovernmental organizations of civil society that tend to have public goals; local, regional, and city authorities; and the private or hybrid organizations that regulate specific sectors through formulating standards (the so-called standard-setting bodies). While this list is not exhaustive, these types represent an important and innovative component of the new world politics. Significantly, the sheer number of transnational enterprises, civil society nongovernmental organizations, and standard-setting bodies has increased significantly in recent decades and follows a pattern very much in line with the spread of globalization. A similar pattern can be identified in the development of the international projection of city and regional diplomacy.

Nonstate players have acquired a growing role in world politics by performing an increasing number of functions. They bring new issues to the attention of the public and in so doing help formulate the political agenda—think of the recent campaign by civil society for abolition of the death penalty. They lobby policymakers, as with the decision to waive the debt of the most indebted countries at the end of the twentieth century. They offer technical assistance to governments and to intergovernmental organizations; for example, many NGOs provided legal help during the conference that led to the Charter of the International Criminal Court of 1998. Both private and public players provide funds; the Bill & Melissa Gates Foundation allocated considerable resources for sanitary projects on a world scale, and the incomes that support those who are fundamental to the functioning of the World Intellectual Property Organization (WIPO) originate mostly from taxing enterprises on their patents and trademarks. They formulate regulatory decisions, such as various codes of conduct and the Kimberly Process that provides guidelines for the trade of diamonds. They implement programs and public policies, as in the whole sector of development aid, but also policies regarding conflicts and the role played by mercenary troops. They provide services, such as private centers for providing visas, which in the past was a sovereign prerogative of embassies. They monitor adherence to international agreements, such as the documents compiled by the most important NGOs on human rights, files delivered to the most important intergovernmental organizations, such as the United Nations. They address disputes—numerous nonstate chambers for arbitration resolve international litigation. They also apply enforcement; many NGOs enhance respect for rules through campaigns to discredit governments and multinational corporations.

A note of caution. The transnational logic of global governance needs to be understood as working in parallel to the traditional state-centric logic, at times in cooperation with it, and at times in competition. The multi-stakeholder logic of global governance is expanding and consolidating, but it is far from replacing the old state-centrism. The resurging unilateral power politics of the last decade is self-evident and yet the global governance logic remains important. These two forces will continue in the future. We need to have a wide enough perspective to understand the world in which we live. This book intends to shed light on the multi-stakeholder realm with a focus on the role of cities and the intersection between state-centrism and nongovernmental action. In the following sections, I expand on the features that distinguish city diplomacy from formal state diplomacy, and on the conditions under which they complement or undermine each other. I also take into account other kinds of relationships, such as those between cities and region, businesses, and international organizations.

Transnational Strategies and Organizational Forms of NSAs

Global politics is played by both traditional governmental actors and NSAs through innovative formats and updated political strategies. Among them, networking, campaigns, and partnerships play a prominent role. To be effective, global political actors need to upgrade their repertoire of action and tactics, accumulating power by aggregating actors from different countries. Cities follow this path, increasingly engaging in transnational networking and campaigning to pursue their city goals beyond their municipal and indeed national borders. As we will see later, city networking is a key feature of city diplomacy.

In global politics, transnational networks play a central role. In this context, a transnational network can be defined as a permanent coordination among actors in different countries, aimed at developing both protests and proposals in the form of campaigns and common mobilizations at both the national and international levels (Marchetti and Pianta 2012). The network is possibly the most common organizational form in the age of globalization. Transnational networks have an extremely important role in aggregating social forces and developing common identities cross-nationally. Transnational networks may be hybrids, including governments, international organizations, multinational corporations, civil society organizations, and local authorities. They may also be sectoral, including only one type of actor.

Transnational networking is a form of organization characterized by voluntary, horizontal patterns of coordination, which are trust-centered, reciprocal, and asymmetrical. Networks are in fact eminently nonstate organizations; two major features of the network's organizational form are its flexibility and fluidity. A flexible organizational structure enhances the group's capacity to adapt to changing social circumstances and political situations at the global level. A fluid organizational structure, conversely, allows for porous organizational boundaries that do not require that enrollment be ratified by formal membership, facilitating work across national and cultural borders. Network structure varies, in that connections can be direct as well as indirect, and linkages can be centralized or decentralized with differing levels of segmentation (Anheier and Katz 2005; Diani 2003). The main activities of transnational networks include spreading information, influencing mass media, and raising awareness. In this vein, they constitute a sort of "global infrastructure" for NSAs. By sharing information, resources, and costs, transnational networks generate value for all their participants in terms of innovation, responsiveness, and mutual support, thus achieving greater legitimacy and power in a positive manner. Lobbying, protest, and supplying services to constituencies are the main functions and objectives of transnational networks.

A network among organizations from many countries forms when a set of preconditions exist in terms of values, identities, and political projects, when a convergence develops regarding the importance of a specific global issue, and when there is agreement on a common issue frame and appropriate strategies to tackle it. The procedures through which consensus on values, identity, and strategy are negotiated, affirmed, and reproduced among independent members that decide to work together on global issues are crucial to achieve convergence. In the process of network formation, a statute, charter or program is usually imperative, which is then approved following different procedures, both formal and informal, consensus being the most frequent method.

Transnational networks are characterized by a set of common beliefs and values that define their political identity (Keck and Sikkink 1998). Transnational networks depend on shared values, and at the same time are key organizational instruments for building mutual trust, identities, common visions, and strategies through continuous negotiations (Risse-Kappen 1994; Schulz 1998). Unlike in the national case, the members of transnational networks do not originally share the same issue frames, political cultures, or repertoires of action, nor do they generally share a language. Within a national context, the common language, culture, and experience make collective action easier, involving both organizations and individuals in a highly informal pattern. At the global level, such common ground cannot be taken for granted and has to be slowly built by the deliberate, long-term efforts of organizations with substantial resources. With global issues, the complexity of the issues and the resources needed to act on them are major barriers to global activism. Transnational networks have represented a major way to lower such barriers and allow broader participation in global campaigns.

Decisions on what strategy NSAs adopt depends on assessing which course of action fits the specific political circumstances in which they navigate. The strategic choice entails balancing specific NSA characteristics (in terms of local conditions, political perspective, experience, know-how, and objectives) and the external environment. Only by establishing a good match between the agent-related and context-related factors can an international activity or mobilization succeed. Essential in this is good timing (as with the pro-Tibet mobilizations that coincided with the 2008 Beijing Olympic Games or the pro-LGBT protests in the context of the 2014 Winter Olympics in Sochi). The results of an endeavor may end up being very different, depending on the moment in which it is launched. These elements— timeliness and fit between resources and the problem to be addressed— constitute the core of the concept of the political opportunities structure (McAdam, McCarthy, and Zald 1996).

The structures of global political opportunities in which bilateral action and transnational networking take place are complex and multilevel. While the issues that motivate the mobilization can be at times global, as with global warming, the possibility of a successful mobilization is rooted in the structure of the political opportunities that bring together the local, national, and transnational spheres of political action. In local and national contexts, NSAs are based in a dense network of social relations and common identities and have access to important resources (human, financial, etc.), but they operate in highly formalized political systems that constrain their mobilization through a number of political filters. As examined later, the space for city diplomacy depends to a large extent on the institutional framework at the national level.

By contrast, at the global level NSAs face high costs in building transboundary relations with actors with different cultures and languages and have access to limited resources, but they have fewer institutional constraints, and hence more opportunities for action. Thus, the lack of a rigid institutional environment similar to the national one amplifies the possibilities for political action. In different ways, international organizations such as the United Nations or the European Union and the other global governance institutions can provide opportunities to create political space to the advantage of NSAs. For instance, within pluralist networks cities and regions can easily cooperate with international institutions as well as foreign governments, which they struggle to do without the shield provided by international organizations.

In conclusion, certain conditions increase the chance that NSAs will be effective in their global actions. Recent studies have demonstrated that transnational activism has greater efficacy when the following conditions are satisfied: (1) transnational coalitions and networks exist on specific global issues, and NSAs participate from different action areas, as well as the academic community and the business world; (2) different forms of actions are used simultaneously (such as campaigns of public awareness, protest, lobbying, politics, and alternative practices); (3) a multilevel strategy is adopted (local, national, regional, and global) that runs parallel to multilevel global governance using the various windows of opportunity that such a strategy offers; (4) "vertical alliances" are created with agencies of the United Nations, friendly governments, and actors of the business world through the support of the gatekeepers and the annihilation of the veto-players and other opponents of the campaign; (5) global events that raise visibility and provide opportunities for the exchange of ideas and practices take place, such as meetings of the United Nations; (6) there is strong leadership characterized by charisma, passion, acumen, and determination; (7) resources such as funds, personnel, and information are available; and finally (8) institutional obstacles are few or absent (Pianta, Ellersiek, and Utting 2012; Scholte 2004).

In all these environments that had been traditionally reserved to diplomatic relations, the relevance of these NSAs is growing. We live in an age in which power is spreading in thousands of channels inside societies. Politics has become an art that is increasingly difficult to practice, requiring the ability to play on more levels and to interact with many different actors in a very short time. NSAs are a permanent element of any action of global politics, and city diplomacy needs to be understood in this context.

2 • A World of Cities

Demographic and Economic Trends

Cities can be understood in at least three different ways: (1) As populated areas. We use the term *urbs* to refer to areas where people live and work, as the term is used in geography and urban studies. (2) As societal compounds. We use the term *civitas* to refer to an aggregation of citizens; this is the term as it is used in sociology and economics. (3) As institutional aggregations. We use the term *polis* to refer to a form of government, as in political science and law. In this book we tend to focus on the third meaning of cities, while we take the other two taken into account from time to time as integral parts of the discussion. In this book, the "city proper" refers to the administrative boundaries of the city—the actions of city diplomacy are carried out mostly by its administrative structure. At times, when politically understood in this way, cities are also referred as noncentral governments (NCGs), a term that also applies to other local authorities such as provinces.

An *urban area* is considered to be a human settlement with high population density and an infrastructure of built environment, unlike rural areas made of small villages and the natural environment at large. Quantitatively speaking, what counts as a city varies significantly from country to country: what we define as cities according to the criteria of the US Census Bureau or other national offices for statistics may or may not apply elsewhere. However, conventionally we can define cities as urban centers with more than 50,000 inhabitants. Anything smaller would be a town, village, or a hamlet. Cities are classified as *small* if they are between 50,000 and 100,000 inhabitants. They are considered *medium* if they are between 100,000 and 250,000. They are *big* if they are between 250,000 and 500,000. They are *extra-large* if they are 500,000 to 1 million, and they are *extra-extra-large* if they are between 1 million and 5 million. They are considered *global* cities if they are above 5 million and have a significant level of international connectivity. *Mega* cities are cities with more than 10 million inhabitants. They usually include metropolitan areas larger than the city itself, strictly speaking.

While an *agglomeration* consists of a central municipality and its suburbs (that is, a continuous urbanized area), a *conurbation/metropolitan area* is a larger urban cluster comprising a core city plus satellite cities, towns, and also rural land that are socioeconomically connected through economic social ties, employment, and commuting. In history and at present, there are also *city-states* or *micro-states*. This is an exceptional case of conflation between the form of the city as a subunit of the state and the state territorially reduced. These entities are internationally recognized states, and no longer retain the nature of local governments (e.g., the Holy See, Singapore, or Monaco). Such city-states have entirely collapsed into the state, and they do not reflect the duality that characterizes most cities in the world. While some perceive this typology as the ideal normative arrangement for international affairs, a world in which states disappear and are totally substituted for by cities, this is not the normative underpinning of the present book. Here I focus on cities as subunits of larger systems, be they national or macroregional.

Cities are traditionally interpreted as different from other social aggregation not only in quantitative but in qualitative terms. The topos of the city as opposed to the village is a recurrent theme in sociopolitical analysis as well as literary reflections and other artistic forms. The contrast between the styles of urban large aggregations and the rural small communities has been central to much modern reflection on social life. In the village, the sense of community and the social bond tend to be much stronger, but with the process of urbanization we witness a process of individualization, if not atomization. Modernity, with its disruptive impact on traditional customs, brings about a radical transformation of human development characterized by more freedom of choice, but also more uncertainty. At the same time, urban modernity amplifies the reach of social interaction beyond the traditional place-based, circumscribed life. It is thanks to the resources made available in the city context that individuals are able to expand their sociopolitical and economic reach internationally. Cities become interlinked to the international projection and become the hubs of transnational connections. But prior to that stage, they also serve as cultural centers for the development of civilizations.

Cities, in fact, can also be conceived of as a cradle of cultures. A fascinating interpretation provided by Davutoğlu links cities to civilizations. He argues that capital pivot cities are "the spatial reflection of cities' civilizational consciousnesses" (Davutoğlu 2021, 35). While it is clear that through-out human history, the city has been the focal product of population, tech-nological exchange, economic relations, division of labor, and institutional development,

> beyond a certain stage, cities that have become supra-generational civilizational melting pots subjectivize themselves and turn into subject-spaces that shape the generations fostered within them. A collective conscience, collective consciousness and collective mindset developed within this continuum turns a city into a driving force of history independent of the people living in it. What subject could have had more impact on Greek philosophy than Athens, on the Roman order than the city of Rome, on the early Islamic renaissance than Baghdad, on Ottoman civilizational blending than Istanbul, on the birth of modernity than Paris, on industrial society than London, and on the transition from modernity to globalization than New York? (47)

Cities have expanded and become increasingly powerful within global dynamics (Borja and Castells 1997; Derudder, Hoyler, Taylor, and Witlox 2012; Khanna 2016; Knox and Taylor 1995; Massey 2007; Sassen 2000, 2001, 2002, 2004). This phenomenon can be regarded as the result of two well-established features in today's world: urbanization and globalization. The world's urban population has grown rapidly since 1950, from less than 750 million to 4 billion people (United Nations 2018). Half of the world's population is therefore already urbanized, and by 2050 it is expected to reach over 6 billion—roughly 70 percent of the entire world population. In 2018, there were 1,860 cities with at least 300,000 inhabitants, 598 cities with between 500,000 and 1 million inhabitants, 467 cities with between 1 and 5 million inhabitants, 48 cities with populations between 5 and 10 million, and 33 megacities with more than 10 million inhabitants (United Nations 2019).

The "urban turn" of the twentieth century has been developing consistently and will continue to do so in the upcoming decades, along the following four lines: (1) there will be a shift from Europe and the West to Asia and then Africa; (2) small and medium cities will grow; (3) there will be an explosion of *megacities* with more than 10 million inhabitants; (4) less-developed regions will grow at an accelerated rate (United Nations 2019). The ranking of the largest cities in the world has dramatically changed over time. In 1950, "only" 12 million people earned New York City the top position, but today the conurbation Tokyo-Yokohama is first with a population of 37 million.

What is striking in the current group is definitely the predominance of cities from the emerging economies of Asia: Jakarta in Indonesia, Delhi and Mumbai in India, Seoul-Incheon in South Korea, Manila in the Philippines, Karachi in Pakistan, and Shanghai in China. The only exceptions are New York City, which now ranks only ninth, and São Paulo, Brazil, in the tenth position.

By 2030, the size ranking is estimated to change again. Tokyo should maintain the leading spot, while new entries are expected from Asia (Beijing, China, and Dhaka, Bangladesh), Africa (Cairo, Egypt, and Lagos, Nigeria), and North America (Mexico City). Delhi is expected to soon become the most populous city in the world. But the real trend in the next few years should be the rise of megacities with over 10 million inhabitants. As of today, there are 36 megacities in the world, with 41 predicted by 2030. Two-thirds of the world's megacities today are in Asia, in countries at different stages of development ranging from Japan and China to India and Indonesia, but also South Korea, the Philippines, Pakistan, Iran, and Turkey as well as Thailand, Bangladesh, and Vietnam. The remaining megacities are located three each in North America (in the United States and Mexico), South America (in Brazil, Argentina, and Peru), Europe (in Russia, France, and the United Kingdom), and Africa (in Egypt, Nigeria, and the Democratic Republic of Congo). Scrolling down the list, Europe ranks low, even if we include Russia and Turkey. Europe does not have megacities; even if metropolitan areas are considered, its cities remain quite small compared to their ever-growing counterparts from Asia and Africa: Moscow, 16 million; Istanbul, 13 million; Paris, 10 million; London, 10 million; Madrid, 6 million; Berlin, 5 million; Rome, 4 million.

Beyond the mere demographic dimension of the world cities, their economic function as hubs of globalization is the most important feature of *world/global cities*. A certain consensus formed from the 1990s identifying as global cities primarily London, New York, and Tokyo (Knox and Taylor 1995; Sassen 2001; Taylor 2004). While the origin of the term "world city" dates back to Goethe, who defines as "Weltstadt" both Rome and Paris, which were during the eighteenth and nineteenth centuries the most important centers of culture of the world (Gottmann 1989, 62), today's understanding of global cities is much more centered on the economic dimension, and the list of global cities is becoming much more Asian. To count internationally, cities must be globally renowned, whether for banks and money or for culture and popularity. Economic and soft power can be considered key assets for the internationalization of cities.

The push for neoliberal globalization of recent decades has had the effect of supercharging global financial markets, simultaneously empowering multinational corporations and disempowering states, which started to retreat from many of the tasks of determining economic activity. In addition, the digital revolution dematerialized space, connecting faraway places in a matter of seconds. The process contributed to the creation of global hubs such New York, Hong Kong, and London that assumed the role of global infrastructures, transnational hubs for the global market and the global village.

Approximately 80 percent of today's world GDP is based in cities (World Bank 2019); the top 600 cities with a fifth of the world population generate 60 percent of world GDP (Dobbs et al. 2011). While urban territory amounts to only 2 percent of total lands, the urban agglomerates have a disproportionate weight in the global economy. A number of other indicators also confirm the centrality of cities in socioeconomic processes. Cities consume around 60 percent of global energy consumption, generate 70 percent of the total greenhouse gas emissions, and produce 70 percent of global waste. Cities have larger budgets than many states and corporations around the world. The GDPs of New York City and Tokyo top the national GDPs of medium-sized countries such as Spain, South Korea, and Canada. Mexico City's and São Paulo's GDPs are each almost bigger than the combination of two countries such as Finland and Israel. Tokyo's GDP approaches one-third that of the entire Japanese economy.

Among the most globalized cities, there are not only big and high-income municipalities, but also middle- and lower-income cities as well as medium-sized and small cities (Beall and Adam 2017). While they are not financial nodes, they represent centers of production and consumption of services, and hence are important hubs of globalization. While the traditional global cities were primarily New York, London, and Tokyo, along with Paris, Frankfurt, Zurich, Amsterdam, Sydney, and Hong Kong, the emerging "world cities" include newcomers such as São Paulo, Mexico City, Mumbai, and Seoul. The JLL Cities Research Centre suggests a trifold taxonomy of cities aimed at measuring economic performance (JLL Cities Research Center 2015):

(a) Established World Cities are highly globalized and competitive metropolitan economies with the deepest and most settled concentrations of firms, capital and talent. This would include the "Big Six" "super cities": London, New York, Paris and Tokyo, more recently joined by Hong Kong and Singapore.

(b) Emerging World Cities: business and political capitals of large or medium-sized emerging economies that function as gateways for international firms, trade and investment. This category includes the likes of Shanghai, Beijing, Istanbul and São Paulo. However, in this group, shape and growth are uneven: Shenzhen, Dubai and Bangalore, for example, are globalizing at breakneck speed; Jakarta, Manila and São Paulo are making notable improvements in key competitiveness measures; but other cities, like Dhaka, struggle to cope with global change.

(c) New World Cities: these are small or medium-sized cities that have an attractive infrastructure and strong quality of life, and deliberately specialize in a limited number of global markets. Brisbane, Melbourne and Boston are archetypal "New World Cities." Many possess high-tech, innovation or research capabilities, such as Vienna, Munich and Tel Aviv. Others like Barcelona, Berlin, Miami and Cape Town are cultural entertainment and tourist hubs. The majority feature at the top of the various "quality of life" and "sustainability" indices and [have] had notable success in attracting fluid capital, companies and talent (see for example Auckland, Copenhagen, Vancouver and Vienna).

Arguably, this tumultuous growth of cities will not be significantly affected by the recent COVID crisis. While the role of the state has clearly been stressed in the response to the health crisis, it is once again in the cities that the problem became more acute and needed to be addressed. Granted, the coronavirus has hit the infrastructure (public transport) and attractions (theaters, museums, concerts, sports events, restaurants) very hard. Zoom has demonstrated that work does not have to be undertaken in expensive central cities. And the growing inequality in cities, part and parcel of the drawbacks of globalization and class polarization linked to wealth production (Sassen 2014), has narrowed inclusion in local politics and may well push the same sort of flight to the suburbs by more affluent whites that occurred in the 1960s, especially in relation to the recent unrest in the US context. And yet, while the COVID crisis may reinforce trends already under way and could partially transform the nature of the cities, I do not expect a significant U-turn in the process of urbanism and internationalization that has characterized city development in the last decades. This book disputes the argument that the COVID crisis, or growing economic inequality, or technological innovation may reverse the powerful urbanization and internationalization dynamics taking place at the city level. On the contrary, I argue that urbanization will continue and this will also significantly impact the landscape of national politics by strengthening the liberal/globalist camp insofar as most electoral results show an overall predominance of liberal majorities in big cities. This also explains a certain resistance from conservative parties to such process of urbanization, beyond their traditional orientation to the countryside life.

From World Cities to Urban Archipelagos

The *world city* notion formulated by Friedmann was crucial in linking urban processes to global economic development (Friedmann 1986). It consists in a set of hypotheses about the spatial organization of the new global division of labor. The first "functional thesis" states that the identity of the largest metropolitan areas is determined by their connections in the world economy, and hence by the functions they play within the latter. Friedmann refers to three major functions of such cities: headquarters functions, financial centers, and points of connection between national (or regional) economies and the world economy. Only the most important cities perform all three functions together. The second "hierarchical thesis" interprets cities as sites in which corporations organize production and plan marketing through a hierarchy that differentiates primary cities (such as Tokyo, New York, Singapore, and São Paulo) from secondary cities (such as Seoul, Buenos Aires, Caracas, and Milan), depending on features such as their prominence as centers of finance and the number of headquarters, international institutions, and inhabitants they include. This distinction is further clarified via a core/semiperiphery dichotomy. Additionally, for Friedmann, world cities also perform the function of global control, as reflected in the structure and dynamics of their production sectors and employment in such areas as international finance, insurance, communications, and advertising. Within these cities, the composition of employment is bipartite, with highly specialized professional workers and low-skilled labor. World cities are major sites for the accumulation of international capital and points of destination for large numbers of both domestic and international migrants. Finally, according to Friedmann the world-city formation brings into focus the major contradictions of industrial capitalism such as spatial and class polarization. In this context, social costs grow at rates that tend to exceed the fiscal capacity of the state, and the allocation of the budget tends to reflect the equilibrium of power, which tends to favor the upper classes (Friedmann 1986). World cities are therefore conceived of as the ultimate centers of power over the production and expansion of the market. Crucial factors are their mode of integration in the global economy and the spatial dominance assigned by the capital to the city, which can be global, multinational, national, or regional. Cities are centers through which money, workers, information, commodities, and other economically relevant elements flow, connecting adjacent areas into the global economic system. World cities can therefore be conceptualized as organizing nodes of the global economic system. This view is particularly important since it provides a new image of intercity relations that transcend state boundaries (Friedmann and Wolff 1982).

The global cities notion as developed by Sassen takes stock of Friedmann's hypothesis on world cities and adapts it to the context of globalization (Sassen 2001). From her perspective, global cities are the first global service centers in urban history. Current economic globalization is characterized by the geographic dispersal of economic activities, and the consequential simultaneous integration of such activities. These phenomena increase the growth and relevance of central corporate functions centered in global hubs. The complexity of these central functions requires subcontracting to specialized service firms, which that tend to concentrate in particular areas where information and services are readily available. This concentration is a consequence of the complex nature of the services they supply, the uncertainty of markets, and the importance of speed in business. Such firms tend to concentrate in strategic sites—global cities—since they benefit from access to large amounts of information, knowledge, speedy transport, good communication infrastructure, and innovative environments. Last but not least, these global cities usually provide a fairly good quality of life (including political and economic stability) and can attract high-skilled workers from abroad, such as managers, professionals, and diplomats.

Networks of cities emerge from the increasing diffusion of affiliates or from some other type of partnership. From an analytical point of view, Sassen disconnects the strategic functions of the global economy (enshrined in global cities) from the overall business economy of a nation-state. Specifically, she considers the former to be partly embedded in the latter as well as constituting a distinct corporate subsector. While Friedmann's world cities were considered separately from one another, according to Sassen there is no such thing as a single global city; such cities derive their significance from the network itself, which in turn constitutes the real space of power in the global economy. Cities are therefore conceived as nodes in a transnational network that links the economically most advanced parts of global cities. In this way, the wealth of cities is detached from their hinterlands and national economies and remains directly networked to the global transformation processes (Sassen 2000). Intercity relations are governed by specific principles of horizontal organization (Taylor 2012b). The relations between actors in network systems are ruled by the principle of cooperation, while the relations in hierarchical systems are characterized by dependency and competition (Powell 1990). Intercity relations mostly consist of networks governed by cooperation and mutuality. Every city requires the presence of other cities, and all of them support the prosperity of the network itself. This explains the difference between Friedmann's hypothesis of a global urban hierarchy, in which world cities struggle to expand their special dominance, and all the literature that follows Sassen and the interlocking-network model.

Nevertheless, cases exist in which some sort of vertical relations can occur in the intercity relations. Taylor highlights at least three circumstances (2012b). The first occurs when the political process dominates relations within the network. The example provided is the modern world in which nations-states have territorialized social space, resulting in the strong national urban hierarchies that were prominent in the twentieth century. The second circumstance is the so-called "gateway battle" that occurs when the economic capacity of one region or state allows just one city to act as point of connection ("gateway") between the region or state and the rest of the world, as with São Paulo replacing Rio de Janeiro or Toronto replacing Montreal as the cities leading national economics. The third circumstance refers to historical cycles. Cities tend to follow economic cycles, period of prosperity followed by economic downturns. In periods of growth cities cooperate to mutually improve their economic wealth; in periods of decline, competitive forces rise. That is what happened in the late Middle Ages in northern Italy in which only four cities, Genoa, Milan, Venice, and Florence, survived as independent actors.

These three sets of circumstances are not inevitable. It is in fact the behavior of agents that leads to hierarchical pressures. Taylor concludes his argument with the case of Chinese Hong Kong. When sovereignty over the city returned to the People's Republic of China, the majority of analysts thought that Hong Kong's economic power would dramatically deteriorate. It was thought that Shanghai would become the new point of connection between China and the world city network, whereas it was believed that Singapore would become the economic pivot of Pacific Asia. Surprisingly, that did not happen; Hong Kong grew tremendously, and so did Shanghai and Singapore for a number of years. Recent turbulence suggests, however, that the future may see a different trend.

From an historical point of view, cities have arguably always existed in a system of connections, constituted by material flows, information transfers, or other sorts of economic linkages (Beaverstock, Smith, and Taylor 2000). No city has ever developed without trading with the external world (Jacobs 1969). A city has always implied a group of cities entangled in trade relationships. Before globalization, these world cities were hubs at the centers of their region of interaction, and their intercity flows correlated with their population. However, such relations boosted and expanded at a global scale with the revolutions in telecommunications and information technology, which are the roots of economic globalization. In consequence, cities today are economically interrelated, dependent and interdependent within a framework of economic networks as broad as the whole planet (Taylor 2004).

Nine historical *regional city networks* can be identified (Taylor 2012a): five of them were in East Asia (mostly in China), two in the Mediterranean region, one in Europe, and one followed the intercontinental extension of the Muslim Empire during its golden age. Taylor considers only networks composed of at least ten world cities with more than 80,000 inhabitants, and networks that lasted a minimum of 200 years. The first East Asian city network, the very first one in our history, developed in China and lasted from the fifth century BCE to the first unification in 221 BCE under the Qin dynasty, during a period of increasing urbanization. This network included the cities of Linzi, Xiatu, Luoyang, Daliang, Yiyang, Qufu/Lu, Yenhsiatu, Shangqiu, Xinzheng, Handan, Suzhou, Anyi, Yong, and Yianyang (listed in order of increasing population size). The second one occurred during the last period of the Tang dynasty in 700–800. It included Changan, Luoyang, Guangzhou, Suzhou, Chengdu, Xin Jang, Youzhou, Kaifeng, Nara, Kyoto, Lhasa, and Wuchang. The third existed between the Mongol Yuan dynasty and the Ming dynasty (1300–1400), and it connected several cities, including Nanking, Hangchow, Peking, Kamakura, Canton, Kyoto, Soochow, Sian, Seoul, Kaifeng, Wuchang, Yangchow, Fuchow, and Chuanchow. The fourth occurred in 1500–1600 (including Peking, Osaka, Kyoto, Hangchow, Nanking, Canton, Sian, Soochow, Seoul, Chengdu, Sumpu, Changchun, Fuchow, Kaifeng, and Yamagushi) and the fifth in 1700–1800 (including Peking, Canton, Yedo, Hangchow, Osaka, Kyoto, Soochow, Sian, Seoul, Kingtehchen, Tientsin, Fuchow, Foshan, Chengdu, Nagoya, Lanchow, Shanghai, Ninghsia, Changsha, Ningpo, and Kaifeng). The first Mediterranean network developed from 200 to 100 BCE when Republican Rome dominated the region. It connected Alexandria, Rome, Carthage, Pergamum, Antioch, Jerusalem, Ephesus, Apamea, Cibyra, and Syracuse. The second spread during the Imperial era (200–300) and linked Rome, Alexandria, Antioch, Carthage, Capua, Ephesus, Pergamum, Apamea, Caesarea, Smyrna, Mazaca, Trier, Milan, Emerita, and Nicomedia. The Muslim City Network emerged in 900–1000 and spread from the Iberian Peninsula to Central Asia. It included Baghdad, Cordova, Fustat/Cairo, Samarkand,

Alexandria, Nishapur, Basrah, Samarra, Kairouan, Bokhara, Mopsuetia, Al Ahsa, Seville, Isfahan, Tinnis and Ravy. Last but not least, the only very European world city network developed in 1500–1600, as a consequence of the first sparks of the process of modernization. This network connected Paris, Naples, London, Venice, Seville, Prague, Milan, Potosi, Palermo, Rome, Lisbon, Ghent, and Madrid.

The first evidence of *intercontinental city networks* can be found in the period between 1250 and 1350 (Abu-Lughod 1989). At that time, the system of trade in goods between Europe and Asia became more integrated than ever before, establishing a transcontinental world system in which cities were the most economically powerful components. The author identifies a vast "archipelago of cities" composed of eight intersecting regional networks connected by trade relations. In the northwest section of the archipelago we find Bruges linked to Genoa and Venice. This merely European network was connected with Asia through three routes: a land route that began in Constantinople, a sea route from Cairo, and a land route from Damascus, which then linked with Baghdad, from which two alternative east routes began. One was a land route heading to Peking through Tabriz and Samarkand, and the other one a sea route heading to Hangchow through Aden, Calicut, and Malacca. In Abu-Lughod's system, the cities in the middle played the role of exchange centers. It is for this reason that the author opts for the noun *archipelago* instead of *network*. This world archipelago collapsed with the spread of the Black Death epidemic during 1340s, which halted most trades between West and East.

World city networks emerge in the modern era. Castells' consideration of world city networks is embedded in the overall explanation of the structure of the relationships that underpin contemporary societies. According to him, these societies operate in a space articulated in flows (flows of capital, information, technology, organizational interaction, image, etc.), which generate networks. "Networks constitute the social morphology of our societies" (Castells 1989, 500). The appearance of such a pattern of social relations is associated with the modern age, especially with the revolutions of communications and information technologies, which allowed the interaction of distant people, and of economic globalization, which led to the widening of the scale, scope, and intensity of any social interaction. This new social configuration developed in several stages, one of which led to world city networks. In Castells' view, a new space is composed of flows instead of places. Global networks are connected by cities (the nodes), and their relations occur at different intensities and at different scales, integrating regional and local centers at the global level. The connections occur through flows of information, people, knowledge, and ideas. Like Sassen, Castells believes that cities are perpetually connected to the network, and they acquire their significance from the network itself. Yet Castells moves further, extending his focus to a larger number of small and big cities, beyond the few "leading cities" of Sassen.

Interlocking networks are particularly integrated city networks. The current world city networks can be interpreted as structured by three main elements: (1) at the level of network stands the world economy, in which services are dispensed; (2) at the level of nodes stand cities, which provide the knowledge for producing services; and (3) at the subnodal level stand business-service firms, which produce and deliver services (Taylor 2004, 2014; Taylor et al. 2009). To sum up, the world economy is the net, cities are the nodes, and firms the subnodes. This specific configuration of network, in which nodes are connected through their subcomponents, is called an interlocking network. The reason Taylor introduced this new level of subnodes reflects the fact that cities (the nodes) are not thought to be the prime agency in forming and reproducing the world city network. Instead, he draws attention to other agents, namely business-service firms that deliver services on a global scale and have therefore allocated offices in cities all over the world. Thus, the formation of a world city network emerges from the aggregate of the worldwide location strategies of major advanced producer-service firms. In other words, the essence of intercity relations has to be seen as an intrafirm office network. Despite his major focus on business-service firms, Taylor points out that the latter are not the only agents that have globalized their work through workplaces in many locations. Indeed, he presents other examples of interlockers, such as the United Nations through its agencies, states through their diplomatic missions, and NGOs and media through their offices. All four agents can complement business-service firms in the interlocking network. The most connected cities in terms of UN agencies are Geneva, Brussels, Addis Ababa, Cairo, and Bangkok. The cities with more diplomatic missions are Washington, DC, Tokyo, London, Paris, Rome, and New York. The most integrated cities in the NGOs are London, Geneva, Washington, and Nairobi, and the global media networks are Manila, London, New York, Paris, Los Angeles, and Milan for the latter.

In addition to networking, the other important characteristic of cities is their porousness. Cities have become more permeable than in the past precisely because they are enmeshed, to a greater extent, into transnational and indeed trans-city flows. People, money, goods, pandemics, ideas, and weapons all get in and out of cities easily. The susceptibility of cities to extranational intrusions has thus become the hallmark of the global cities' literature.

City cannot be sealed off; they trade and interact with other cities across national lines, leapfrogging above the bureaucracy and politics of their respective nation-states. In this vein, cities cannot be conceived of as self-isolated entities; rather, they are elements of fluidity constantly exposed to external influences but also able to influence other external actors.

Urban archipelagos are a specific, intense form of clustering. Compared to the previously examined networks, archipelagos occupy a reduced geographical space. Connectivity is a key factor in cities' fast-growing role in the contemporary world (Khanna 2016), and global cities are expanding even more thanks to developments in transportation, energy, and communication, a huge international infrastructure of a million kilometers of roads, railways, pipelines, and wires that connects and mobilizes people, resources, information, and money, on top of airports and harbors. The powerful combination of connectivity and urbanization then produces urban archipelagos, vast clusters of cities that stretch over hundreds of kilometers. The following examples give a sense of the notion of urban archipelagos: Japan hosts the biggest city cluster in the world: Tokyo-Nagoya-Osaka, with eighty million people and a major share of the whole Japanese economy. China and India follow closely, with clusters growing around Beijing, Shanghai, Hong Kong–Guangzhou, Delhi, and Mumbai. On the northeastern coast of the US over fifty million people live and work in the area from Boston to Washington through New York City and Philadelphia. The counterpart on the West Coast is located between Los Angeles and San Francisco and of course includes Silicon Valley. The Johannesburg-Pretoria area accounts for one-third of the South African GDP and hosts the continental offices of big multinationals. The Cairo-Alexandria corridor in Egypt is where almost all the population lives and most economic activity takes place, while the new cluster Lagos–Benin City is growing on the Atlantic coast. Other relevant urban archipelagos include Teheran and Istanbul (with their surroundings), the Abu-Dubai area in the Emirates, and Greater London and the Rhine-Ruhr region in Europe. All of these regions thrive on connectivity, mobility, flows, and exchanges; it is estimated that by 2030 there will be about fifty such urban archipelagos worldwide.

The reasons the engines of globalization tend to concentrate in urban archipelagos are rooted in several urban features that make them the most suitable and profitable sites for the production and the exchange of goods, services, and capital. First, cities are centers of highly concentrated human capital—which is in turn attracted by the urban provision of good infrastructure and amenities. This implies that a wide range of labor is available, from low-skill workers to well-educated, specialized workers, and there is also substantial demand for all sorts of products, from manufacturing to services and finance. Second, cities are centers of good transportation infrastructure and connectivity; there may be advanced means of transport such as high-speed trains, international airports, and well-equipped commercial harbors, and often high-speed internet is available. These features reduce distances, help business, facilitate movement of information, cut the costs of producing and transporting goods, and reduce the costs for financial transactions. Third, cities are centers of innovation and knowledge. The concentration of human capital enhances occasions for interaction and communication, especially among educated and specialized individuals. These dynamics facilitate creative thinking, promote innovation, produce spillovers of knowledge, and spur the elaboration of new projects and ideas. The spread of knowledge is facilitated by the presence of advanced telecommunication facilities, the possibility of accessing information channels, and the presence of centers of research and institutions of higher education. Finally, cities are characterized by a closer access to politics, as administrative and governance institutions tend to concentrate there.

Today's global affairs are shaped significantly by global cities (Acuto 2013a; Massey 2007; Oosterlynck et al. 2018; Sassen 2001). With their populations and economies growing, urban centers have witnessed a rise in their global power (Ljungkvist 2015). Cities are increasingly active internationally. Cities do what the *comuni* (i.e., Italian city-states such as Florence, Venice, or Genoa) used to do for many centuries (Guidoni 1992). In some areas, this is particularly evident. As the past regional policy commissioner of the EU, the Austrian Johannes Hahn, put it, "Cities, not nations, have been the main players during most of our civilization's existence, and cities may again overtake nations as the primary building blocks of Europe. Cities have to be at the heart of our plans to create a Europe that is prosperous, environmentally sustainable, and where no citizen is marginalized" (cited in La Porte 2013, 85). Global cities almost exert a "command-and-control function" in today's world (Acuto 2010, 430), based on soft power that allows cities to deploy persuasive influences on economic, financial, social, and cultural processes.

Cities both influence and are influenced by the processes of globalization. Not only are they active in hosting global flows of goods, services, people, money, and information, they are objects of the policies of international institutions such as the United Nations, the World Bank, and the International Monetary Fund, and also of big private corporations. Not only do they influence human relations and lifestyles, they absorb and enforce global norms and rules. Globalization has transformed cities into strategic places of intermediation in contemporary world relations. The global economy, in particular, has made cities crucial hubs in a worldwide grid of complex networks that go beyond national borders and the old divides such as North and South or developed and developing countries. Global cities are now located both in the North and the South of the world (or rather in the "global North" and in the "global South"), and they are the actual spaces where globalization processes take place. They are platforms for international flows and provide goods and services, in addition to being important gathering and meeting places that connect and facilitate social interactions and cultural exchanges.

The direct consequences of the concentration of the economic forces of globalization in cities is their large proportion of wealth and population. As mentioned earlier, at present, cities contribute some 80 percent to the world's GDP (World Bank 2019). Moreover, 55 percent of the global population lives in urban settings (World Bank 2019), a share that is expected to grow to over 60 percent by 2030. Narrowing the focus to the 300 largest metropolitan areas, the latter contribute to 49.1 percent of world GDP, 24.1 percent of world population, and 23.3 percent of world employment (Brookings Institution 2018). In addition, cities have become the most important component of national economies. In both developed and developing countries, they produce a disproportionately high rate of economic growth compared to the countryside. For instance, in 2011, Tokyo and London—with respectively 26.8 percent and 20.3 percent of the total population of Japan and United Kingdom—accounted for 34.1 percent and 26.5 percent of their countries' total GDP. Another impressive case is Dublin, which with 25.9 percent of population produced 32.8 percent of the Irish GDP (United Nations Human Settlements Programme 2011). The same dynamic occurs to an even greater extent in developing countries. For instance, in 2008, Buenos Aires produced 63.2 percent of Argentina's GDP with 32.5 percent of the population. Nairobi, with 9 percent of Kenya's population, generated 20 percent of its GDP. Shanghai, Manila, Brasilia, Cape Town, Karachi, and Nairobi produced GDPs more than 100 percent higher than their population share; in Addis Ababa this percentage is more than 360 percent. The most impressive cases are Kinshasa and Kabul, which generated more than 500 percent higher GDP than their population share (United Nations Human Settlements Programme 2011). Also in terms of economic growth, the most internationalized cities are outperforming their respective countries. The more the city grows and becomes internationalized, the more its economic growth will flourish.

Part II • City Diplomacy

In their increasing presence on the world stage, cities have emerged not only as centers and driving forces of the global economy, but also as political actors in global affairs (Acuto 2010, 2013a, 2013b; Acuto et al. 2017; Amiri and Sevin 2020; B. Barber 2013; Chan 2016; Curtis 2014, 2016; Gutierrez-Camps 2013; Hocking 1993; Hocking et al. 2012; Leffel 2018; Terruso 2016; Tuirán Sarmiento 2016; Van Der Pluijm and Melissen 2007; Viltard 2010). They are not only places in the world economy, they also play a political role by actively engaging to craft defined positions and pursue their specific interests, to address common issues and contribute to setting the international agenda, and to influence law-making processes at the highest level of global governance and monitor their implementation. This broad phenomenon, known as *city diplomacy*, is a product of several factors.

The significance of municipalities in world politics has grown in parallel with the gradual weakening of the traditional, state-centric framework of international relations. The modern Westphalian system came out of the Peace of Westphalia back in 1648; it later consolidated with the Congress of Vienna (1815) and was codified through the Vienna Convention on Diplomatic Relations (1961). This international political order is based on sovereign nation-states, with defined boundaries and responsibilities and exclusiveness as international actors. In such a scenario, diplomacy consists only of state-to-state relations, and foreign policy is monopolized by national governments and ministries. For centuries international affairs have developed with laws and institutions, rules and practices designed by, and for, nations themselves.

In recent decades, new actors have informally entered the diplomatic stage. Diverse in nature, size, purposes, and tools, they mostly belong to three categories: civil society organizations, multinational corporations, and local authorities (regions, provinces, cities). In a new configuration of international politics, these rising actors aim to fill a governance gap. They are generally referred to as nonstate actors, but among them local authorities differ in some ways. First, their territorial dimension differs from the nonterritorial, transnational scale of civil society organizations and big corporations. Second, they have a substate nature, neither full nation-states nor nonstate subjects like NGOs, social movements, or multinational companies. Local authorities are still institutional entities, however; they are part of the public administration and enjoy a certain degree of sovereignty, although at a lower level than the central state.

Traditional diplomacy was a competence exclusively held by the official institutions for foreign affairs of the state—the foreign ministry and the diplomatic service officials. This was due to the characteristics of the international system, in which states were the only actors entitled to engage in international relations, the only legitimate representatives of the people. The Vienna Convention on Diplomatic Relations of 1961 codified the rules of diplomacy. Article 3 indicates the functions of the permanent diplomatic missions, which include the following goals: representing the state, protecting its citizens and interests, negotiating with foreign governments, elaborating reports on the internal activities of foreign states, promoting friendly relationships, and incrementally building economic, cultural, political, and scientific collaboration between the two countries. Ambassadors and consuls were expected to send to the state regular reports on the host state's activities, and when relations harden or grow tense, the foreign ministers first and the heads of state on a few occasions used to meet to declare their positions or to search for a negotiated solution. Unlike today, embassies were the outpost of diplomacy, and the Foreign Ministry was a sort of big eye keeping all aspects of international relations under control.

Today the exclusivity of traditional state diplomacy is challenged on two different accounts: normative and functional. Normatively, citizens demand more participation in international affairs, since international affairs influence them more directly. From this perspective, the city certainly has easy access to this entry point to international affairs. Functionally, on the other hand, the effectiveness of state acting alone is questioned in a pluralist and complex context. In such situations, additional actors can have a significant impact on global dynamics. City diplomacy is emerging as an obvious and effective route to the international empowerment of citizens.

A number of contextual conditions favored the emergence and consolidation of the international role of cities (Marchetti 2016). Current global governance arrangements allow for the participation of a number of different political actors considered to be relevant stakeholders in what were previously closed government rooms (Hale and Held 2011; Higgott, Underhill, and Bieler 2000). The growing recognition of the principles of subsidiarity, stakeholder participation, decentralization of power, and local self-government have provided robust normative support for the role of cities. The transformation of authority from its traditional understanding in terms of institutional delegation, to one based on the relevant actors' expertise, principles, or simply capacity to deliver made extra room for claims from local authorities (Avant et al. 2010). Additionally, global transformations have generated cross-cutting issues such as global warming that became more intrusive in local politics, and hence required an increased level of local legitimation, which could obviously be found more easily in the city context. The globalization process also generated a sense of common purpose among civil actors, triggered internal unification and an increasing the sense of solidarity and empowerment (Van Rooy 2004). For the first time, a number of ad hoc coalitions and campaigns have been organized on a transideological basis, going beyond the traditional political barriers of previous forms of national mobilization and targeting a number of controversial aspects of globalization. Also, technological innovations in the information technology field revolutionized organizational patterns within civil actors (Hill and Hughes 1998; Warkentin 2001). Through the internet, actors from different parts of the world have been able to increase their political know-how and their ability to join forces transnationally, addressing common targets. Moreover, changes in social behavior, such as the proliferation of higher education and the expansion of international travel, have empowered citizens. Through the diffusion of higher education and mass travel, an enlarged group of activists have been able to get in contact with their potential constituency. The spread of knowledge and the building of new transnational trusty relations provided the bases for mobilization (J. Smith and Wiest 2012, 168). In this newly evolved diplomatic context, cities have certainly taken advantage of the space left unfilled by states. New "glocal" threats as well as transnational opportunities have provided the right incentives for the international mobilization of cities.

The domestic features of the urban context also matter for city diplomacy. The concept of cityhood encompasses some specificities that are crucial in defining the international activism of cities: proximity, concreteness, and flexibility. Cities indeed are close to people; they are the setting in which we experience everyday issues. To find practical solutions, they count on a pragmatic, on-the-ground approach, one that must provide concrete outcomes. In cities, local politics is conceived and lived: people meet, gather, and debate in public spaces, and they enjoy more direct participation and control than they do in national politics. Municipal governance is also more accountable to its citizens, rapidly and directly, and the relation between electors and elected is thus stronger. Urban politics is "street-level politics": it is more visible, more inclusive, and less formal than at the national level, and the urban space itself easily accommodates political activities, in streets and squares where citizens can dialogue, demonstrate, and build platforms and identities. As a result, the "get-things-done" spirit of municipalities is largely appreciated by citizens, who value efficient, tangible outcomes to daily problems much more than faraway summits and talks among state ministers and delegations. In what Chan calls "subgroupism," citizens shift part of their loyalties from nation-states to close-at-hand collectivities, and prefer the concrete action at the local level carried out by city leaders (Chan 2016). Mayors in particular usually enjoy more trust from citizens than national politicians: often independent and nonpartisan, they are perceived as pragmatists, problem-solvers, and real civil servants (Barber 2013). This asset of public trust provides a substantial boost to the international activities of the mayors.

In addition, cities tend to be more "sovereignty-free" rather than "sovereignty-bound" as states are (Chan 2016). Freer from sovereign obligations, cities can act more flexibly, overcome ideological constraints, and concentrate on designing and implementing practical solutions. States have more formal responsibilities and obligations that limit their room for action. This is a particularly critical point for the international activities of cities. While they enjoy an edge of freedom due to their "informal" status in international affairs, they aspire to a more formalized recognition in global governance. But this could turn out to be a double-edged weapon—it would increase their formal bargaining power, but at the same time decrease their room to maneuvering because their formal visibility is limited. While formal recognition of their international status may have long-term strategic benefits, it also imposes tactical costs on cities. Hence, whether to seek formal recognition of their international status remains a key strategic dilemma for the future of city diplomacy.

The phenomenon of city diplomacy struggles to find a place in the traditional theoretical frameworks of international relations, which tend to ignore the subtleties of subnational-national-international interactions. In addition to the rather recent origin of the phenomenon itself, the theoretical difficulty in the conceptualization of the city diplomacy phenomenon is mainly due to the dual nature of the diplomatic action of the cities. In fact, these substate entities operate at a diplomatic level in two distinct spheres, national and the international. While in the former the legal rules that apply to the city's diplomatic activities differ from state to state, in the latter, cities have no legal agency.

Scholarly attention to city diplomacy emerged in the 1990s (Aldecoa and Keating 1999; Alger 1990; Duchacek, Latouche, and Stevenson 1988; Hobbs 1994; Hocking 1993; Soldatos 1990). As examined in previous chapters, attention to the international dimensions of cities in the global economy was already significant in the '80s, the specific focus on city diplomacy being consolidated only later. In the '90s, the international action of substate entities was called "paradiplomacy," and was mostly intended as a direct continuation, to varying degrees, of state foreign activities. The focus of research was different, however, in North America and in Europe. In the US, the origins of the concept of city diplomacy are to be found in studies of "foreign municipal politics" forged in the late '80s around the study of social protests against the conservative and neoliberal policies of the Reagan era (N. P. Smith 1988). These reflections on municipal foreign policies are rooted primarily in the sociology of political mobilizations. This research aimed to interrogate the skills of local authorities in the international field and the legitimacy of these new local mobilizations against federal administration foreign policy. In this perspective, the focus was often on community-based initiatives, bringing together various substate entities, NGOs, citizen groups, and local governments working together to promote peace and global development (Lofland 1993; Shuman 1986, 1992). The origins of the European's concept of city diplomacy is to be found in the field of decentralized cooperation institutionalized by the state, rather than in social protest movements (Hafteck 2003). The issue of city diplomacy emerged in the context of the debates on decentralized cooperation (regions, cities, NGOs, etc.). Indeed, decentralized cooperation, together with other topics, remained a major field of operation for many European cities (Cochrane, Peck, and Tickell 1996; Le Galès 2002).

3 • Structural Factors of City Diplomacy

City Diplomacy: Definition and Trends

The basic definition of city diplomacy understands it as the combination of institutions and practices that allow urban centers to engage in relations with a third party—a state or NSA—beyond their borders, with the objective of pursuing their interests. On a formal hierarchical scale of diplomatic engagement, city diplomacy occupies a lower position than state diplomacy, but a higher one than citizens' diplomacy and civil society activism. It is lower than state diplomacy because it has no formal mandate, but it is higher than citizen activism because it is institutionalized and often backed by electoral mechanisms. While in a classical understanding of international affairs state diplomacy is considered to be the primary form of government-to-government interaction (Hamilton and Langhorne 2011), citizens diplomacy (Sharp 2003) and the transnational mobilizations of civil society organizations (della Porta and Tarrow 2005) are usually considered uninstitutionalized forms of international activism. City diplomacy, with its legitimacy warranted by electoral mechanisms, its formalized institutional structures, and its closeness to citizens, constitutes an intermediate level of international engagement, sitting between states with full political institutionalization, a formal international mandate, and low proximity to decision-makers, and civil society organizations, with low political institutionalization, an informal international mandate, and high proximity to decision-makers through the inputs directly advanced by the people (table 1).

City diplomacy has been interpreted and consequently labeled differently. Some have argued that this diplomacy has developed in parallel with classical state diplomacy, and so should be defined as "paradiplomacy" (Aldecoa and Keating 1999; Tavares 2016). Others call it municipal foreign policy (Leffel

Table 1. Modes of International Engagement

	High political institutionalization	Low political institutionalization
Low proximity to citizens	States	Corporations
High proximity to citizens	Cities	Civil society organizations

2018) or substate or subnational diplomacy (Criekemans 2010). State and city diplomacy can be seen as two parallel routes: city diplomacy does not replace the national—it is separate, yet additional and subsidiary. City diplomacy may be seen as representing a further case in the decentralization of international relations management by nation-states. In particular, it can be understood as producing a vertical fragmentation of national foreign policy, while the horizontal process typically occurs in the context of international organizations, where it is shared with other states. While these definitions tend to assume a clear division of labor, the reality is that the scope of competences is subject to continuous bargaining and competition between the central administration and city authorities. The two actors tend to operate in a complex multilayered system in which competition and cooperation alternate.

City diplomacy takes different forms to adapt to the different institutional settings and political opportunities within which it develops. While in rigid Westphalian states city diplomacy tends to be entirely ancillary to official foreign policy and to have derivative power only, in "postnational" or "cosmo-national" states, city diplomacy is usually warranted much stronger legitimacy, which derives from below and is linked to the transnational networks of peoples and businesses that tie one city to another. In the present study, city diplomacy is understood, then, as a general definition that includes different types of applications and models. I selected the concept of "city diplomacy" over the others that appear here and there in the literature—paradiplomacy, microdiplomacy, municipal foreign policy, transnational municipal policy, municipal internationalism, municipal diplomacy—as a general concept that can take different shapes according to specific political circumstances. In particular, I use the term "city diplomacy" rather than "paradiplomacy" because the latter is often used with reference of regional diplomacy. While city diplomacy and regional diplomacy share a number of characteristics, this book is about city diplomacy only. It is also important to state here that the phenomenon of city diplomacy remains centered on a shift from international relations to global politics rather than simply representing a different way of constructing or deconstructing the field of practice.

And yet, city diplomacy is not actually an entirely new phenomenon. The international activism of cities even predates the existence of nation-states. In the past, and well before Westphalia, big cities already acted as foreign policy entities. In ancient times, for instance, Athens and other Greek city-states would send and receive envoys to one another to negotiate political and social issues. During the Renaissance, major cities such as Venice and Florence had diplomatic networks that included permanent missions abroad. Several other cities across Europe and Asia have a long tradition of exercising political, commercial, cultural, religious, and military power on a vast territorial scale, including Rome, the German cities of the Hanseatic League, Genoa, Cairo, Istanbul, and Baghdad, and Chengdu in China. With the modern age and the Westphalian order, cities were marginalized by the rising nation-states and their bureaucracies that encompassed diplomatic activities.

In the decades after World War II, municipalities discovered (or rediscovered) their international agency along three lines. First, cities became "informal" actors in the dynamic of the Cold War. Several cities in the East and West managed to build links that proved important for the unfolding of the social and political reconciliation after the collapse of the Berlin Wall. Second, cities and other local authorities played a growing role in global governance. Thanks to the growing public debate on global issues, the demand for more direct participation pushed both citizens and local officials to seek more active involvement in international affairs. Third, bilateral cooperation developed in many different fields, such as the decentralized cooperation between the cities of the French Fourth Republic and the German Federal Republic in the 1950s and '60s (van Overbeek 2007). This process of devolution of powers and competences from the central state to local authorities has taken different forms and modalities according to the internal characteristics of the state in question. While in the various European national experiences, city-to-city cooperation has arisen mainly from bottom-up initiatives linked to cooperation, in the US case, town "twinning" has had—in contrast to its civic origins—its push from programs implemented by the federal government[1] according to top-down dynamics (Bontenbal and van Lindert 2006).

Important in this trend is the recognition that internal decentralization allows the public administration to better manage local problems. From this follows the idea that there is a direct correlation between local development and decentralization. Since the decentralization of powers is perceived as the most effective internal management mechanism of the territory, the decentralized cooperation between local governments, even across national borders, comes to be perceived as an additional tool in the hands of local authorities to manage issues at the international level. In this way, a fundamental connection is formed between internal decentralization and external decentralized cooperation. In summary, what emerges from this historical evolution is the (re)birth of the ability of cities to entertain external relations, eroding the monopoly of the state at the international level.

In understanding city diplomacy, we should not repeat the errors made for too many years when studying state diplomacy. For a long time, state diplomacy was conceived exclusively with reference to states as actors, objects, and instruments. Then came the realization that NSAs can also be objects and instruments of state diplomacy. We should apply this lesson also to city diplomacy. While we need to have a minimum level of institutionalization in terms of actorness, we should not expect city diplomacy to be enacted only peer-to-peer and only through civil servants (contra, e.g., La Porte 2013 and others). Diplomacy can be developed through different tracks that have as objects and instruments actors other than local authorities. This way, municipalities should be understood as carrying out international activities, at times directly engaging citizens of other cities, without necessarily entering a formal relationship with local or national authorities. Similarly, city councils can deploy individuals, civil society organizations, or private companies as proxies to promote their interests abroad, without necessarily making use of their official civil servants. We can distinguish between "city-to-city" relationships, i.e. only between cities, and relationships between cities and other international actors—cities to governments, cities to international organizations, cities to businesses, and cities to citizens. In addition, it is possible to distinguish the various diplomatic actions of the cities based on the number of actors involved. There are two-sided activities where only two agents are involved, and also multisided actions in which several actors participate. Finally, it is possible to distinguish between diplomatic activities aimed at extracting benefits for a single actor and those that produce distributed or collective benefits.

Cities in Global Governance

With the emergence in the international sphere of the external actions of local authorities in general and of cities in particular, a link is formed between internal and international politics in which the line of demarcation between the two becomes increasingly blurred (Putnam 1988). In "polylateralism," that is, the transformation of the international arena itself into a mix of relations between state, nonstate, and substate actors (Wiseman 1999), the border between domestic and foreign policy is becoming less and less clear, and the dividing line between the actions of official actors and those of unofficial actors is increasingly blurred. On the one hand we find the state, an official actor in international relations, whose actions have been recognized and regulated by the Vienna Conventions on diplomatic and consular relations (in 1961 and 1963, respectively) and that continues to have a privileged role in foreign policy. On the other hand, we find the city, which although it lacks official responsibilities in the international arena such as those of the state, nevertheless appears to be an integral part of public administration and claims considerable political legitimacy resulting from local elections. In other words, while the gap in the regulation of the diplomatic activity of local authorities has not yet been filled by international law, and often not even by the laws of individual states, the city's legal "belonging" to the institutional system of its own state, and the political legitimacy of its municipal government through the electoral process, place the international activity of the local authority in a political-juridical limbo between the official and the unofficial.

The hybridization of contemporary international politics weakens the separation between domestic and foreign policy. State-centered diplomacy is accompanied by a second multicentered paradiplomacy characterized by a pluralism of actors that includes local authorities. In the era of globalization, the evolution of international politics is generating a transition from a strongly state-centric international system, with a clear separation between domestic and foreign policy and clear regulation and legal standardization of interstate relations, to a continuum of types of policies, in which different elements of the internal and international political sphere, in different subnational, national, or international political arenas, are mixed together to produce a multilevel diplomatic environment (Hocking 1993). The international environment is multilevel precisely because of the combined presence of actors located on different political levels. In this, the different actors claim institutional legitimacy on the basis of their electoral mandate, their actual powers, and their competencies, degrees of autonomy, and resources. Ultimately, the international system should be seen as a transnational network environment in which nonstate or substate actors operate simultaneously across multiple scales (Betsill 2006). Cities play an important role in global governance both singly and through networks, both bilaterally and in multilateral, multistakeholder settings (Aldecoa and Keating 1999; Alger 1990, 2010, 2014; Amen 2011; Amen, Toly, McCarney, and Segbers 2011; Bouteligier 2012; Chan 2016; Duchacek et al. 1988; Hobbs 1994; La Porte 2013; Le Galès 2002; Lecours 2002; Zheng 1994).

The Legal Dimension of City Diplomacy: National Trends

The legal environment in which cities operate internationally can be divided into two main domains: national and international. At the national level, the relationship between the national government and local authorities is undergoing significant transformations in terms of enhanced cooperation in some cases and of growing competition in others. At the international level, legal documents continue to marginalize the international status of cities, and yet in practice cities are gaining increasing recognition for their role. It is worth examining both domains in detail.

The national differences in the agency of cities—that is, its legal standing and administrative role—is very noticeable. For instance, unitary and federal systems are quite different legally and politically with regard to cities. In the United States, for example, cities are not mentioned in the US Constitution, and in constitutional law, cities are legally "creatures of the states," as Judge Dillon pointed out in a railroad case in the state of Iowa, which was decided in the Iowa State Supreme Court in 1868 and later upheld by the US Supreme Court. In Italy, cities, provinces, and regions are constitutionally established as local authorities with a certain degree of political autonomy: cities have administrative and fiscal but not legislative power. In practice, state constitutions are more or less restrictive in giving cities different powers; we call the more restrictive states "Dillon's law states" and the more permissive states "home-rule states." In theory, all states allow some sort of home rule for cities, but in a number of states this home rule is limited to the largest cities. Thus, the national legal setting does matter for determining what a city can or cannot do beyond its borders; despite both being global cities, London and Los Angeles, for example, do not have the same sort of legal powers because they are embedded in different legal systems.

The question of the constitutional powers of major cities is going to be a key issue of democratic governance for the next half-century. Should the growing significance of cities automatically mean that they should be empowered? Looking at this tension from a strategic perspective, a note of caution is needed here. It could be the case that precisely because cities are becoming too powerful, their power will be constrained by actors who have an interest in the status quo. This has to do with the cleavage between cities and the countryside and their political representation. In many countries, including Canada, the UK, and the US, conservative parties derive a significant portion of their support from rural areas whereas liberal parties tend to be majority in big, globally integrated cities. In these cases, the greater constitutional power of cities and greater representation of urban areas in national legislatures, together with the growing urbanization process, would curtail the power of rural areas and the likelihood that they could form a legislative majority or governing coalition. Under these circumstances, conservative parties could argue that greater urban representation might lead to a tyranny of the urban (liberal) majority over the rural (conservative) minority, and that national cohesion would consequently suffer. While the final result of electoral competition depends on a many different variables (Bartels 2010), under conditions of growing urbanization process, the city-countryside cleavage may contribute to the strengthening of the liberal camp, thus significantly altering the traditional balance of political power in the long term.

The tension is not only between the national government and city authorities, but also significantly between provincial authorities and city authorities. In the Canadian context, for instance, the question of a new constitutional level for cities has been raised with some frequency and is particularly fraught. At present, cities are particularly dependent on provincial governments, without much intermediation from the federal government. Provincial governments are certainly reluctant to give up such power. The case of Montreal is particularly illustrative. Were the provincial government induced to give way to city autonomy, the move would immediately raise the specter of Quebecois nationalism, since the political culture of Montreal is markedly different from that of Quebec as a whole; a Montreal with a constitutionally guaranteed jurisdiction would be much more reluctant to separate from Canada than Quebec as a whole. The cleavage between city and countryside remains key to the future of political dynamics in many countries and has significant implications for the scope and legitimacy of city diplomacy.

At the national level, four broad categories of interaction between the central government and local authorities can be identified: collaboration, competition, competitive collaboration, and indifference. Since the creation of nation-states, cities have been embedded within the state legal setup. Thus, cities are more or less free to act depending on the character of the state they belong to, the legal treatment they receive from national legislation, and other factors related to the legal provisions of the state. The first domestic restriction is expressed in the highest law of the country, that is, the constitution. Obviously, countries with written and rigid constitutions can expressly limit or devolve power to local governments, unlike common-law states, which are based on interpretation and the jurisprudence of constitutional courts. Basically, national constitutions can recognize the city's international relations, forbid them, or, as happens in the majority of cases, remain neutral, indeed silent. Only a few states permit expressly local authorities to practice diplomacy, among them France, Belgium, and Argentina. A few countries explicitly forbid cities from exercising international relations. The US, for instance, does not allow cities or other local governments to enter treaties, to preserve the unitary national position of the federal state in international relations. A third type of relation falls between the two reported above: a sort of competitive cooperation, where cities and states work jointly in some cases and separately in others. The most common case, however, is the neutral position of the constitution, which occurs when legal rules determining cities' prerogatives of diplomacy are absent or extremely basic. In these cases, cities can take advantage of the vacuum of legislation to pursue their policies of international relations up to the point that the state decides to limit them. Certainly, if cities invade fields that are the exclusive competence of the nation-state, such as national security, defense, foreign affairs, or external borrowing, it is reasonable to assume that their action will be challenged before the courts. However, cities are numerous and hardly monitored by the state, and they can take initiatives that do not always require formal legal arrangements. This can be interpreted as a benefit for cities, because they can work in "alegal" spaces.

Undoubtedly, city action can be part of a nation-state international strategy in a scheme of complementarity with a ministry of foreign affairs (Cabral, Engelke, Brown, and Terman Wedner 2014). When the state can no longer effectively manage certain international issues due to the weakening caused by globalization, it creates opportunities for cities and other new actors to exercise functions previously performed by states. Complementarity occurs in cases where both actors can carve out roles in solving the same problem, but from two different perspectives. An example is the reconstruction of government structures in societies where a war has just ended. By acting complementarily, the government can help reconstruct central government structures and cities can work on local government structures. This would be an example of controlled decentralization, where local entities are empowered to reinforce the state structure, to implement state provisions efficiently and become part of their diplomatic toolkit. In this case, the state does not perceive the city as a competitor or an enemy, because they share the same interests. From the point of view the state, this is foreign policy by proxy. Cities would enjoy a certain space to maneuver while implementing national provisions, and they could be the means through which the state concludes negotiations with external entities. Their capacity to engage in diplomacy depends on their administrative structure allowing them to be the actor engaged in negotiations. When synergy is promoted between the central government and cities, the government can use city diplomacy as an instrument of national foreign policy, and results may be achieved that would have been unattainable without such synergy. An example is the case of Vilnius during the Cold War, which the USSR used as a tool to influence Central and Eastern Europe. Vilnius was also used on the opposite side after 1989 as a tool to create linkages to Western Europe and USA. Similarly, Budapest, in the post-'89 era, was used as a channel to promote EU accession. Recently, the Dutch government established coordination tables with several cities to pursue convergence on several international dossiers.

An interesting instance of national foreign policy by city proxy is provided by the case of Istanbul and its connection to Turkish foreign policy. The Istanbul metropolitan municipality Directorate of Foreign Relations has been very active in organizing a series of programs to foster the city's international projection. Among these, in November 2018, members of the Istanbul Municipal Council visited the Governorate of Tokyo, the Kyoto municipality, and Shimonoseki municipality, with which Istanbul has been a sister city since 1972. The visits came at a very important time for Turkey and Istanbul after an attempted coup led to the invasion of the building housing the Istanbul Metropolitan Municipality. The Istanbul delegation provided information to these Japanese governments on the events and on the accusation about the Gulen movement, integrating national foreign policy with municipal foreign action. The delegation also recalled the long-lasting relationships between Turkey and Japan, celebrated in the 2003 "Turkey Year in Japan," the 2010 "Japan Year in Turkey," and paved the way for the 2019 "Turkey Year in Japan." Ultimately the delegation encouraged different actions to increase the number of Japanese tourists coming to the city.[2]

However, a cooperative relationship between central government and local authorities in foreign policy can become highly political and controversial. The Chinese attitude is a case in point. Last year, Li Xiaolin, president of the Chinese People's Association for Friendship with Foreign Countries, stated that "Sister city relations play an important role in boosting cooperation and exchanges among Chinese and foreign cities under the framework of the [Belt and Road Initiative]."[3] In recent years the activism of Chinese cities has intensified significantly. Chinese cities have by now established 2,629 sister cities and provinces overseas and have formed sister-city relations with more than 700 cities in countries involved in the BRI. Beijing alone is sister cities to no fewer than 21 capitals of countries that have signed on to the BRI. Paradiplomacy and city diplomacy constitute significant components of the current Chinese soft-power strategy. But precisely for this reason, it is getting very controversial. In Czechia, Beijing canceled its sister city agreement with Prague after the city council approved a similar agreement with Taipei. In Sweden, because of the deterioration of the bilateral relations at the central government level, a number of city agreements have been cancelled. In the past year, the cities of Linköping, Lulea, and Vasteras have ended official cooperation deals with Guangzhou, Xi'an, and Jinan. Even more significant is the case of Gothenburg, which decided not to renew the twin city agreement with Shanghai, a symbolic linkage between China and Europe. However, China is not the only country that politicizes these kinds of local agreements. In 2018, the city of Osaka ended its sixty-year relationship with San Francisco after local officials recognized a statue of Japan's "comfort women" erected in Chinatown as public property.[4] Another example is the Istanbul-Rotterdam partnership. The two cities had a sister-city relationship between 2005 and 2017, when it was terminated by the Turkish side. The termination followed the banning of Turkish ministers from holding rallies for diaspora communities in Rotterdam before a controversial Turkish referendum on constitutional amendments. Turkish president Erdogan was actively involved in the decision, as he reportedly asked his prime minister to tell the Istanbul mayor to end the relationship with Rotterdam.

By contrast, there are cases where city diplomacy develops free from the state and even in opposition to national government directives, at times even causing disputes that are difficult to resolve. From this perspective, city diplomacy would be seen as reducing the prestige of national diplomacy, if not threatening it altogether. This situation could derive from the lack of international recognition, as in the case of Barcelona, which developed city diplomacy as a functional substitute for the lack of membership in international organizations, or it can result from the general downgrade of diplomats and ministries at the international level. At times, city diplomacy can be interpreted as a challenge to the established national foreign policy. For instance, this was the case for Zurich, part of the network of European cities that favored drug policies opposed to the prohibitionist policies advanced by the Swiss federal government. Through its Project International de Paris, Paris repeatedly affirmed its global political agency against the French central government. Similarly, Rome, setting up an Office for Peace in Jerusalem in 2002, positioned itself against Italian government intervention in Iraq. More recently, Barcelona took a stance against the Spanish central government, acting as if it were the capital of an independent state. Again recently, when President Trump announced the withdrawal of the United States from the Paris Agreement on Climate Change, one of the strongest reactions came from mayors of big American cities. From New York City to Los Angeles, Boston, Philadelphia, Chicago, Seattle, and New Orleans, a group of sixty-one US mayors affirmed that they would remain committed to the Paris deal and pledged to go forward and work together to reduce carbon emissions.[5]

The so-called "Climate Mayors" become national political actors by both taking a hard stance against the federal government and implementing city policies in stark contrast to the national orientation (e.g., Los Angeles's Mayor Garcetti pledged to reach the zero-emission target by 2050 [Hachigian 2019]). Such a strong response from local officials soon made worldwide headlines not only for expressing outspoken disapproval of the American federal administration, but for referring to an international agreement reached by nation-states to which local authorities (cities, provinces, and regions) were neither official parties nor signatories. Another interesting case of tension between the central government and the city government is provided by London. In the post-Brexit context, London is striving to project an image of an outward city, open for business with Europe and the world at large. The new slogan, "#LondonisOpen," shows London's desire to remain an "internationally competitive and successful city," envisaging itself as a prime global location for business, innovation, and market hubs. Finally, there are also cases, such as the Tokyo situation described later in the section on security, in which the city authority managed to pressure the government into action, thereby fueling international tension with the People's Republic of China.

Finally, there also cases in which city-to-city (C2C) cooperation manages to develop, despite tension in the government-to-government (G2G) relationship. In the last few years, the relationship between France and Italy has experienced many ups and downs, but Genoa and Marseille nevertheless signed a cooperation agreement in 2017. While these two cities are in competition in a number of areas, they decided to join forces to maximize support for bringing back maritime trade from the northern to the southern shores of Europe, taking advantages of the doubling of the Suez Channel. City-to-city cooperation is sometimes easier than government-to-government.

Legal Dimension of City Diplomacy: International Trends

At the international law level, overall recognition of the legal status of cities is very limited. No international treaty or convention of the UN, and almost no decision of the International Court of Justice, mentions the existence of localities or recognizes them as legal entities under international law. And strange as it may sound, the seemingly clear legal principle that denies localities' legal agency in international law is hardly ever mentioned in international covenants, treaties, textbooks, or other documents. As mentioned earlier, the Vienna Convention of 1961 does not regulate cases in which cities rather than states conduct diplomacy. Cities are often in a legal vacuum. This produces ambiguity around the kinds of actions that cities can develop, and tends to downgrade city diplomacy. The absence of local authorities from international law is no more unique than the absence of individuals, groups, associations, or corporations. Chan aptly defined it a "conceptual jail" for cities' international aspirations (2016).

The post–World War II period marked an important moment in the international fate of cities. At that time, there was a hesitation about granting cities international status following what were seen as failed experiments with free cities such as Krakow, Shanghai, Danzig, and Fiume, and internationalized cities and territories such as Tangiers and Jerusalem. Some of these experiments were targeted at solving the problems of ethnic and national minorities that, following the emergence of homogeneous nation-states, found themselves oppressed and in need of international protection. A solution was sought in creating special denationalized areas. Cities where such minorities existed were thus freed from the grip of the state and put under international supervision; other free cities were managed to mediate between countries competing over resources and territories. At the end of the day, however, all proved unsustainable and generated more problems. The experiment of free cities was suspended.

In the post–World War II legal setting, local governments are simply seen as integral parts of their states, although this remains problematic in a number of ways. The nature of the city remains caught in the tension between the bureaucratic and the democratic conceptions of localities. On one hand, the bureaucratic conception envisions cities as an integral part of the state, an administrative subunit. On the other hand, the democratic conception understands local governments to be independent and autonomous corporations, insofar as they are directly warranted by popular vote and hence reflect the will of a local community, a kind of semisovereign democratic entity distinct from and independent of the state. The tension between these two conceptions continues to underpin our political understanding. From this perspective, cities can be seen as normative mediators between individuals and the world, in parallel to state mediation. This should be seen as part of the wider process of state functional disaggregation with transnational reaggregation, as elaborated by Slaughter (2004). This way, cities are not just passive entities on which international duties and powers are imposed. They also take an affirmative approach, initiating and forming transnational law by entering agreements with cities across borders, which, when authorized by their states, might be recognized as part of international law.

International law recently began accommodating cities in various ways that are in clear opposition to the doctrinal lack of recognition as legal entities (Blank 2006). Within the international legal framework, cities are present as objects, enforcers, and subjects of policies and norms. Though cities are not full subjects of international law, they must comply with obligations and duties that their states take on when they sign international agreements. And even though local governments' obligations stem from those of the state, they often carry the burden of such obligations and thus become de facto parties to these covenants. International law burdened localities with duties: cities became objects of global, international, and transnational regulation because the urban context is often crucial to achieving a significant social impact. And having been assigned the duty to enforce international norms and standards, cities also gain influence as political entities on the world political stage.

The United Nations and other international organizations such as the EU have endorsed the agenda of transforming relations between localities and their states, as demonstrated through efforts to promote an agenda of "decentralization" and "subsidiarity." The reconfiguration of the relationships between local and state governments is in line with current ideologies that guide global governance: decentralization, market-based economic reforms, democratization, and community empowerment. A significant number of activities performed by the United Nations Centre for Human Settlements (UNCHS) demonstrate this important transition, whereby localities become objects of regulation and vessels through which various international policies are advanced. The UNCHS—later renamed UN-Habitat—was established in 1976 under the Vancouver Declaration on Human Settlements (Habitat I). However, this originally development-oriented agency later became the main engine for a much more profound shift in how cities have been viewed by international policymakers. Indeed, Habitat has evolved into an international body that promotes the transformation of "human settlements" into independent, empowered actors, bringing them closer to obtaining the status of international legal subjects.

A new international norm of city management is emerging. City activism, together with the growing attention from the UN and other international organizations, is bringing about a normative transformation that might lead in the future to a new legal setting that accommodates cities' claims. The UN took this path to a still greater extreme. In 1998, following Istanbul, the UNCHS and the World Association of Cities and Local Authorities Coordination (WACLAC) published a document, "Towards a World Charter of Local Self Government," that aims to be the precedent for an official United Nations Convention. Here, the evolution of the localist ideology reached a global scale: decentralization became a dominant theme. The principles of subsidiarity, proximity, and autonomy are the most important innovations that appear in the 1998 document. Following other eminent cases of norm emergence (e.g., the UN Conventions on the rights of the children, indigenous people, people with disabilities, etc.), in future decades we can reasonably expect a new UN convention on city management conceived as an instrument for stability, economic development, and human rights.

Many international institutions today have developed engagement forums and specific agendas dealing with city issues. Traditionally, the UN Habitat forum has been the most obvious place for cities to get into global politics, but more and more avenues are opening up. A recent case in this direction is the World Health Organization, which has developed a city health diplomacy agenda as part of its Healthy Cities Network (Acuto et al. 2017). Attention is also growing in the European Union, the World Bank, and many other intergovernmental organizations at the regional and global levels.

Actors, Goals, and Drivers of City Diplomacy

Several different urban actors operate in city diplomacy. A distinction is often made between city diplomacy carried out through formal municipal structures and citizens' diplomacy carried out informally by people individually or through organizations such as business companies, NGOs, or other social groups. We can identify four main types of actors in city diplomacy:

1. Formal representatives such as mayors and municipal officials such as aldermen, councilors, advisors, and urban planners
2. Citizens and civil society organizations such as NGOs, think tanks, foundations, associations, ethnic groups, and charities
3. Economic and business organizations such as private companies, service providers, and corporations
4. Educational and cultural actors such as schools, universities, research centers, museums, theaters, and symphonies

As a matter of fact, many cities have set up departments for international affairs, and the number is growing fast. Among big cities, the ones with such departments are still the exception today. The fact that so many cities are reorganizing themselves internally to create a division to deal with international affairs is evidence that cities are taking their international engagement very seriously. We will see in a moment why they do so, but their ambition to be international actors is a fact.

São Paulo provides a good example of organizational innovation in city diplomacy. The city diplomacy in São Paulo made a leap forward starting in 2001 when Mayor Marta Suplicy's government established the Municipal International Relations Secretariat (Secretaria Municipal de Relações Internacionais, SMRI). The SMRI enhanced the city's international actions, allowing it to share experiences with other cities, organize important events such as the UN Conference on Trade and Development in 2004, and lead important initiatives such as Network 10 on the fight against urban poverty of the URB-AL programme promoting cooperation between the EU and Latin American civil servants working in local authorities (Stren and Friendly 2019). Similarly, the city of Milan developed a sophisticated organizational model, divided into three main departments: institutional relations: governments and cities, businesses, and NGOs; EU affairs; and international cooperation, plus an external agency, "Eventing Milan," dedicated to managing big events and attracting visitors.

In city diplomacy initiatives, different actors should be taken into account. At the urban level, the aforementioned four types of actors are all present. Official representatives, beginning with the mayor, are for obvious reasons predominant, but also relevant are CSOs as well as business and cultural actors. Beyond the urban level, city diplomacy also targets governments and international organizations. Dealing with governments is a minefield, because that domain is traditionally considered an exclusive area of competence for national foreign policy, yet cities engage foreign governments via "soft" means. Engagement with international organizations is easier, insofar as the IOs themselves often encourage and mobilize the cities into participation. Cities can initiate the process of international engagement as agents, and they may also be on the receiving end as the sites of important activity. Both are relevant to the internationalization of the cities, but in different ways. While the proactive side is more significant, the receiving component is still important. Often, the city at the receiving end simply accepts an invitation to become a partner, which reflects the imbalance of power between cities in different parts of the world, and yet that new interaction yields important results.

Cities decide to go global for different reasons. A pragmatic approach might push to address concrete issues and find sustainable solutions that cannot be achieved with local action only. Ambition can lead proactively to innovative international actions with the goal to improve urban performance and global recognition through hard, tangible economic development and soft cultural promotion. Power and prestige can induce mayors to go global to gain visibility and win elections. Idealism can produce offers of solidarity and assistance to other cities in hard times or during their development process. Finally, activism from civil society and the urban community can push toward engagement on certain issues.

Two logics underpin the focus on the city: the logic of efficiency and effectiveness, and the logic of democracy. The logic of efficiency and effectiveness suggests that good city governance is the best instrument to achieve effective social results because of its directness and proximity to citizens. Local management, micropractices, and the principle of subsidiarity are all driving inspirations for the focus on the vernacular as a path to achieve social efficiency. City governance is seen as a key engine of the economic efficiency and development that supposedly come with decentralization and local power. A conception of local governments as private corporations suggests that the main goal of cities is to be financially viable, providing good services to their consumer-residents; at times such a conception may even replace the public-oriented one.

In the logic of democracy, on the other hand, good city governance is seen as the best tool to implement the democratic ideal as an anti-authoritarian move. In this view, localities are instruments for achieving community empowerment and democratic self-determination. In a liberal scheme, a localist ideology sees city governance as schoolhouses for democracy, an element that can transform authoritarian regimes and inculcate democratic tendencies in the population. In this way, the international turn to local empowerment should also be understood as an attempt to destabilize nondemocratic regimes.

This overlap between the logic of efficiency and the logic of democracy in city management generates a weird convergence of both democratic and authoritarian states. While the former support city governance because of its democracy-enhancing effects at home and in transitional countries, the latter support it because of its development-enhancing effects that prove the de facto superiority of authoritarian regimes in delivering welfare to citizens. Normative and functional performances both point to the importance of good city governance, which also entails good city internationalization. While these two logics sometimes run counter to each other, most of the time they are aligned in supporting devolutionary schemes and empowering local governments vis-à-vis central ones (Blank 2006). Part of the success of the notion of city governance has to do with precisely this bizarre bipartisan support from both democratic and authoritarian regimes.

In explaining city diplomacy, the intensity of the international activism of cities has been ascribed to a number of different variables. In the following section, I briefly explain this set of variables. They are not conclusive; we still lack a comprehensive study to test the relevance and validity of such variables and their intercorrelation. Nevertheless, they provide a fairly good indication of the most relevant drivers of city diplomacy.

Inside-Out Variables

Mayor's attitude: The personal determination of the mayor is crucial for a municipality to start cultivating relations with foreign counterparts. It is precisely the fact that city diplomacy is less institutionalized than state diplomacy that gives greater weight to the personal attitudes of city diplomats such as mayors. Especially for smaller cities that often do not have a professional apparatus for city diplomacy, personal contacts between mayors and foreign countries or other people are the main vehicle of the city's international diplomatic activities. Mayors are under increasing pressure to play a *three-level game*: local, national, and global. More than thirty years ago Putnam suggested interpreting political dynamics as a two-level game played between the domestic and the international domains (Putnam 1988). Today, we need to update Putnam's original intuition and start to think in terms of a triple-level or indeed multilayer game. Because of the augmented opportunities, as well as the increased threats, that cities are increasingly confronted with in an era of globalization and interdependence, mayors are quickly learning to play on different levels simultaneously to increase their social, economic, and ultimately political impact. A mayor's willingness is often activated by clear political opportunities for local politicians related to visibility and electoral gains, which in turn are often linked to the following other variables.

Citizens' pressure: City diplomacy can also originate from the bottom-up pressure of citizens' activism, as in the case of nuclear-free cities. This is at times linked to the presence of foreign actors in the urban society or to transnational activist networks (see the next variable below).

Urban society: The presence of foreign actors in a city can have important push effects for city diplomacy. International diasporas, tourists, businesses, religious communities, international experts and diplomats, and others are among the actors who can indirectly motivate a city to engage more in international activities.

Political culture: When a political culture spreads among citizens and political elites such that they are ripe for extracting the benefits of transnational politics, city diplomacy is likely to take place. Political parties, for instance, may have different positions in line with their ideological mindsets—for example, they may be either pro–free trade or nationalists—and thus be more keen or less about getting involved on the world stage.

Historical track record: The historical track record of past international activism by the city generates a sort of path dependency that may lead to more diplomatic actions. At the same time, especially in municipalities in which the level of city diplomacy institutionalization is low, it is not uncommon to lose the historical track record of the international activities once the mayor ends its mandate.

Expediency: City diplomacy might simply be an instrument to better serve city interests. Amsterdam is active in Ghana, Surinam, and Turkey because they are the countries of origin of its migrants. In similar ways, cities engage in conflict resolution in other countries to prevent migration inflows. When the state is unsuccessful or inefficient in serving citizens' interests, cities are called to complement or substitute for the state. Barber, and with him a number of mayors, even argue that cities have a right and a duty to respond to the sovereign dysfunctionality of states, and have a right to govern themselves in the true spirit of self-determination and perhaps of democracy itself.

Resources: Tangible resources linked to finance, human resources, and bureaucratic assets are crucial for city diplomacy. Larger cities can count on richer budgets and more numerous staff for diplomatic work, and it is no coincidence that large cities have more solid diplomacy. This does not mean that smaller cities are less active, but that larger cities generally have a stronger impact on the international political agenda. Also important is the availability of financial and knowledge resources at the individual level. Open-mindedness to the world at the micro level remains crucial. The rise of an urban middle class provides the main source of new activists. Likewise, opportunities for mass travel have given people the opportunity to get to know new realities and to build up new, trusting relations transnationally.

Type of economy: If the city is either locally deprived of essential resources or has a significant export-oriented business community, city diplomacy is more likely to search for international ties to support the international projection of its local economic actors. The globalizing economy makes local polities aware of their potential as strategic places and pushes them to become more responsible for their own economic, social, and cultural development.

Institutional framework and degree of decentralization: The autonomy of a city in foreign policy is also determined by the degree of freedom and decentralization allowed by the central state. A city's degree of constitutional autonomy in international decision-making matters. Because, as we mentioned earlier, the legal framework is often silent on this issue, the political dialogue between the central government and the cities is fundamental. If local interests are satisfactorily represented at the state level, there is less need for cities to engage in diplomacy, and if they aren't, the need is greater. The degree of decentralization and territorial devolution of power implies more or less autonomy for cities, of course: in countries such as Canada and the Netherlands, with strong cultures of devolution, city diplomacy is a widespread practice. In more political terms, the foreign policy agenda defined at the national level is relevant as well: if it privileges soft policies (such as the economy, culture, and development assistance rather than military power), local authorities are more likely to engage globally on the same tracks. As a general trend, states are going through a progressive fragmentation of their sovereignty—either upward or downwards, with power being transferred to regional, continental, or global institutions, to subnational territorial actors, or even to the market.

Lack of national diplomacy: City diplomacy may also serve as a functional substitute for "national" diplomacy when a territory aspires to sovereign independence but still lacks official international recognition: this is the case in Palestinian cities for Palestine and Barcelona for Catalonia. The international delegations of the province of Quebec are a similar case; interestingly, and not by chance, they are officially described as city offices, not as country offices (for example, the Quebec delegation is in London [DGQL], not in the UK). It goes without saying that these cases generate significant international controversies of varying intensities.

Geographical factors: Geographical position matters in facilitating the international role of the cities. Cities close to borders, harbors, or rivers usually develop a more open mindset and a deeper inclination to reach out and connect to the world (like Rotterdam in the Netherlands, Shanghai in China, or Trieste in Italy). The location within the national territory is also influential: being in core or peripheral areas of the country, or being far from or close to important centers, may lead to more or less intense agency on the world stage.

Outside-In Variables

Presence of transnational networks: There are outside-in reasons for the boom of city diplomacy. As this book argues, global politics is increasingly marked by the presence of intrusive transnational networks, which push and force cities to react at the global level for both globalist and local motives. Business networks as well as diaspora networks are linked to the incoming and outgoing migration flows.

The nature of the international system and pull effects by IOs: The nature of the international system has an important effect on city diplomacy. The more inclusive and less strictly intergovernmental the system is, the more likely it is to encourage city diplomacy. Often, local authorities go international because they are asked to do so by international organizations. A typical instance is the strong push by the EU for the europeanization of European regional activities that now receive funding from the EU, that contribute to drafting official EU documents (famously, the EU convention), and that have permanent offices in Brussels. International organizations offer a web of transnational relations and an opportunity for exchange and cooperation, forcefully drawing municipalities into global affairs. The emerging norm of urban governance encourages and legitimizes "going global" in many cities.

The pull effect by other cities: The sheer number of internationally active cities generates a duplicating effect in the city diplomacy attitude of other cities. Mimicking and importing best practices is common. At the international level, moreover, cities tend to act differently from states insofar as they pursue a more collaborative attitude. While states often oppose each other in the international arena, cities tend to interact and cooperate beyond their ideological, historical, or national boundaries. When addressing shared concerns, they are more willing and ready to focus on mutual benefits to deliver substantial outcomes to their citizens. The likelihood that cities will develop an international presence depends on the availability of opportunities for cooperation with other cities. Cases of competition, such as the race to host big events or the headquarters of big organizations, definitely exist, but overall remain secondary.

Table 2. Explanatory Variables for City Diplomacy

Inside-out	Mayor's attitude
	Citizens' pressure
	Urban society
	Political culture
	Historical track record
	Expediency
	Resources
	Type of economy
	Institutional framework and degree of decentralization
	Lack of national diplomacy
	Geographical factors
Outside-in	Presence of transnational networks
	Nature of the international system and pull effect by IOs
	Pull effect by other cities

In the past decade, the role of information and communications technology (ITC) in city diplomacy has significantly increased. Digital diplomacy has become one of the multiple ways in which city diplomacy expresses itself. The technological innovations in the IT field have revolutionized organizational patterns within many local authorities and more generally for any sort of transnational activism (Hill and Hughes 1998; Lipschutz 1992; Olesen 2005; Warkentin 2001). Through the internet, cities from different parts of the world have been able to familiarize themselves with other political realities, like-minded organizations, and alternative forms of action. In this way, they have been able to increase their political know-how and their ability to join forces transnationally to address common targets and develop bilateral projects. It is through the internet that a significant portion of the political, cultural, and economic activities that will be presented in the next chapter are implemented. Being able to immediately reach its own citizens as well as the citizens of other municipalities has given an extraordinary opportunity to the most internationally ambitious cities.

4 • Fields of Operations of City Diplomacy

City diplomacy consists of different types of activities. While economic activities are often the most visible, the other types are equally relevant for the impact they can generate for the city. In this chapter I survey the different dimensions of city diplomacy, dividing them by sectoral specialization. I begin with the more political and institutional activities and continue with activities on business and brand management; culture and environment; peace and security; and human rights, migration, and development. While this analytical differentiation may help the reader to systematize the complexity of city diplomacy, it is often the case that several dimensions are at work in a single action or mission abroad.

Politics: Global Governance, Twinning, Networks, and Mega-Events

The first field of action for city diplomacy is political and institutional engagement with foreign counterparts. This consists of bilateral and multilateral interactions with foreign cities, foreign governments, international institutions, foreign companies, foreign civil-society organizations, and international networks. These are the actions of city diplomacy proper. It is through institutional relationships with these actors that cities can set up the bases on which further collaboration can be developed, which is why I begin the chapter on fields of operation of city diplomacy with them. Perhaps counterintuitively, the hosting and organization of mega-events can be not only a lucrative business (under certain conditions), it can more significantly constitute a major vector of public diplomacy. That is why I examine such events in this section on political institutional actions.

At the level of multilateral global governance, institutional engagement entails participating in and influencing the decision-making process at a supranational level. Like state diplomats, city representatives want to defend their interests in international forums. Although less empowered, city diplomats act both within and outside of existing political structures. Within international organizations, cities aim to participate directly in the development of decision-making. This happens in the Committee of the Regions of the European Union, which in addition to producing its own resolutions on specific subjects, has strong influences on the EU Commission and Council on the execution of European policies, given that these often affect social, political, and economic areas that have to do with cities. Institutional representation includes participating in high-level consultations to influence global policymaking processes (lobbying, mainly at the UN and EU levels), but also formally representing the city in important circumstances such as signing ceremonies for an agreement, official visits of a head of state, or international summits. When they instead act outside of existing political structures because they lack the entitlement and status to have an official say, cities practice external lobbying. This happens, for example, at the United Nations, where the United Cities and Local Governments (UCGL) or other city networks are often interlocutors of the UN agencies or the committees of the General Assembly. These city lobbying activities require that individual interests be collected and expressed in one voice, to be more effective in influencing the institutions involved. This entails generating a two-level process, the first among the cities belonging to the network, and the second between the network and the institutions.

Participation in global governance dynamics is not without difficulties and accidents, and cities need to develop an adequate set of internal capabilities to fare well in the global context. Certainly cities face difficulties in entering the international diplomatic circles: they confront relatively inflexible global hierarchies, they must attend to daunting organizational and technical issues, and they risk upsetting local political arrangements (Beauregard and Pierre 2000). And yet, despite these considerable obstacles, cities are developing more and more effective skills for navigating global politics.

The *UN-Habitat* format represents the most advanced domain of global governance in which cities play a prominent role. The United Nations Centre for Human Settlements—later renamed UN-Habitat—was established in 1976 under the Vancouver Declaration on Human Settlements (Habitat I). However, this agency, originally development-oriented, later became the main engine for a much more profound shift in how cities have been viewed by international policymakers. Indeed, through Habitat II (1996, Istanbul) and Habitat III (2016, Quito), Habitat has evolved into an international body that promotes the transformation of "human settlements" into independent, empowered actors. The latest focus of Habitat III was on sustainable urbanization and the "new urban agenda," which are expected to serve as policy guidelines for urbanization planning for the following twenty years. Deriving from the post-2015 development agenda, the discussion was centered on goal 11 of the "sustainable development goals": "Make cities and human settlements inclusive, safe, resilient, and sustainable." The new urban agenda envisions four key mechanisms for reaching this goal: (1) national urban policies promoting "integrated systems of cities and human settlements" in furtherance of "sustainable integrated urban development"; (2) stronger urban governance "with sound institutions and mechanisms that empower and include urban stakeholders," along with checks and balances, to promote predictability, social inclusion, economic growth, and environmental protection; (3) reinvigorated "long-term and integrated urban and territorial planning and design to optimize the spatial dimension of the urban form and deliver the positive outcomes of urbanization"; and (4) effective financing frameworks "to create, sustain and share the value generated by sustainable urban development in an inclusive manner" (Habitat III, 2016). Also central is smart urban planning, in which the rights of the city are emerging as a fundamental entitlement.

The *U20 Mayors Summit* format represents another interesting case of global governance engagement. Urban20 is an engagement group linked to the larger G20. The U20 is a city diplomacy initiative that brings together cities from the G20 member states and observer cities from non-G20 states. U20 members are primarily mayors and their designated sherpas from G20 cities, in addition to invited representatives of non-G20 cities. Each U20 city represents a major economic and political powerhouse. Together, the U20 cities are larger than the fifth-most-populous country in the world; they are responsible for over 8 percent of the global GDP, and collectively constitute the world's third-largest economy, after China and the United States. The U20 aims to discuss and form a common position on issues from climate action to social inclusion, integration, and sustainable economic growth. The objective of the U20 is to bring urban issues to the forefront of the G20 agenda. This objective is pursued by delivering a final communique of recommendations to the G20 president and heads of state.

The U20 uses a structured task-force approach. Each of three task forces focuses on a U20 priority area agreed on by the collective U20 body; they consist of city representatives as well as knowledgeable partner organizations. Over the course of the year, task forces write white papers and policy briefs laying out specific, actionable solutions. These recommendations are then shared with G20 leaders via the U20's final communiqué. The U20 was launched in 2017 at the One Planet Summit in Paris by conveners C40 Cities and United Cities and Local Governments. The first subsequent U20 Mayors Summit took place in Buenos Aires the following year; Tokyo hosted the second in 2019 and Riyadh hosted the third in 2020. The final communiqué of the Riyadh U20, just released on October 2020, was centered on the following items: (1) partner by investing in a green, just post-COVID-19 recovery; (2) safeguard our planet through national-local collaboration; (3) Shape new frontiers for development by accelerating the transition to a circular, carbon-neutral economy; and (4) empower people to deliver a more equitable and inclusive future.

On a regional level, the *Union for the Mediterranean* (ARLEM) and the *Eastern Partnership* (CORLEAP) are equally interesting formats. The EU's Committee of the regions' two joint assemblies are composed by local officials, and both represent a further expression of city diplomacy covering actions in the EU's neighborhood. ARLEM is a unique space where Israeli and Palestinians mayors work together; CORLEAP is a unique body where Belarus local representatives are active in a multilayer political context. Such standing gatherings of several local authorities reinforce the concept of city diplomacy, which otherwise could turn to be volatile, depending solely on the specific political profile of the mayor rather than his or her administration and related structured services. In addition, multilateral bodies such as ARLEM or CORLEAP are officially recognized by institutions composed of member states, which gives city diplomacy additional international recognition.

At the bilateral level, institutional relations have to do with decentralized cooperation between local governments in the mutual exchange of skills, know-how, best practices, and experiences in purely administrative sectors such as mobility, urban planning, bureaucracy, health, welfare services, and other local public services. The element of mutual benefit for the parties involved in decentralized cooperation is what distinguishes this dimension of city diplomacy from classical development assistance. While the latter aims to improve the conditions of a certain community, city diplomacy relates instead to types of decentralized cooperation that produce benefits for all of the cooperating parties. Although these city diplomacy activities may appear to resemble those in the economic dimension, they constitute a separate analytical category. Diplomatic activities of an economic nature take place through the allocation of goods; that is, they are subject to market dynamics; exchanges in the dimension of institutional relations, however, do not concern economic goods, or at least they are not exchanged as such. On the contrary, city cooperation does not produce direct or quantifiable benefits for the cities involved; it is, rather a mutual exchange of administrative expertise, aimed at optimal management by the local authorities of the cities themselves.

Often cities set up their own subsidiaries to manage international affairs, be they political, economic, or social. International affairs have become so important for cities that they find it more expedient to rely on semipublic entities that have more room to maneuver thanks to their greater autonomy from public regulations. An interesting example is New York City Global Partners, Inc., a nonprofit organization housed in the New York City mayor's Office for International Affairs. Similarly, Toronto set up its International Alliance Program that is focused on economic, cultural, and cross-cultural community development. Milan (Eventing Milan) and London (London & Partners) have their own agencies, but they are mostly focused on the business dimension. At times, such activities have been interpreted as part of a wider trend of privatization of public life, which in this case would entail privatization of city diplomacy (Curtis and Acuto 2018).

Since their first engagement in international relations, modern cities used the cooperative model to strengthen their relations with national or foreign localities. A good example of multidimensional international activity is city *twinning* (Laguerre 2019). In the past, in a less globalized world, the largely municipal functions of a city required a focus on the day-to-day business of running infrastructure and utilities, restricting international engagement to geographically close partners or to the activity of sister-city and twinning activities. Today the legacy of those sorts of initiatives, while now considered arcane, continues to facilitate policy exchange—particularly between established and emerging market cities. The origins of sister-city partnerships can be found in the post–World War II policies of the US and UK in a drive to encourage exchanges to foster greater peace and prosperity. For instance, after World War II, Coventry in the UK was twinned with Dresden in Germany as an act of peace and reconciliation, both cities having been heavily bombed during the war. In both the UK and the US, many cities during this period also engaged not only with each other but with more distant capitals across Asia.

Over time, twinning has evolved from basic friendship pacts to complex partnerships that include nearly all the dimensions presented above. City-to-city cooperation was a common strategy to enhance a city's international profile and global competitiveness through generating connections between cities and facilitating the exchange of information, ideas, investments, and people. Those earlier bilateral relationships between cities were linked to several factors, including mayoral or trade relationships, historical or demographic connections, common challenges, or a common faith.

Twinning is linked to the concept of hospitality. There are hundreds of examples of city-to-city cooperation, and many initiatives of sister cities involve young people and students, reflecting a desire for future reinforcement of the persistent links between the two localities. In the past, twinning (or another relationship between sister cities) was mostly aimed at expressing solidarity and reciprocity with friendly cities, but throughout history, and with the end of the Cold War, the practice shifted its focus toward economic development, which the two engaged cities pursue through processes of mutual understanding and friendship, touching on a variety of themes and institutional and noninstitutional actors. Twinning can entail numerous heterogenous initiatives and policies, such as sharing funding, the transfer of knowledge, and sharing responsibilities and leadership (Jayne, Hubbard, and Bell 2011). Twinning agreements are signed, but of course they can also be unsigned. This took place in the aforementioned case of several Swedish cities, including Gothenburg, which recently decided to stop its thirty-four-year-old twinning agreement with Shanghai, after the deterioration of the bilateral relationship between Sweden and China.[1]

City diplomacy is not limited to large cities. Small cities can see the benefits of investing in international monitoring and activities too. The city of Modena in Italy, with a population of 184,727, developed its city diplomacy within the European framework starting in 1995, when the municipality decided to activate Project Europe (Progetto Europa), dedicated to European policies and the international promotion of the city. The objectives of the project were mainly two: supporting Modena's municipality in applying for European funds to develop projects in different policy fields, and putting the city in the international system. The project has since increased in both activities and staff, and it is now called the European Project, International Relations, and Coordination Complex Projects Office (Ufficio progetti europei, relazioni internazionali e coordinamento progetti complessi). As of today, the city of Modena has ongoing agreements and twinning programs with thirty-two cities and regions and is an active member of more than ten city networks.[2]

The objectives of this bilateral diplomacy between local governments are various: development assistance for cities in developing countries, promotion of good practices, sharing values, and cultural, social, or economic exchanges (de Villiers 2009). Formally speaking, we should distinguish "friendship cities" and "sister cities," even though sometimes they have the same meaning. The latter is a broad-based, long-term partnership that is turned into an official relationship through an agreement signed by the highest elected or appointed officials of both local governments. An example of such an agreement is the twinning between the city of Rome and the city of Washington, DC, signed by the two mayors in 2013. The model of "friendship cities" is less formal than twinning, and in some cases is considered a preliminary stage toward city "sisterhood." However, city sisterhood and twinning models of partnership are extremely diverse, reflecting citizens' decisions regarding the intensity of the desired relationship. If the example mentioned above concerned the contract between the two "first citizens" of Rome and Washington, the example of Sister Cities International (SCI) illustrates greater involvement in terms of decision making for both the private sector and civil society. SCI, perhaps the most cited case of city-to-city cooperation, is a nonpartisan, nonprofit organization founded in 1956 by then-president of the US Eisenhower; it gathers sister cities, sister counties, and sister states in the United States, but it accepts also sisterhood between US and extracontinental cities.

Bilateral city diplomacy can at times spark significant controversies, as it did in the cases of London-Caracas and Istanbul-Sarajevo. A controversial plan for city twinning between London and Caracas was reported by Beall and Adam. In 2006 the then-mayor of London, Ken Livingstone, planned a city exchange with Hugo Chavez, the president of Venezuela.

In return for offering transport, planning and tourism advice to Caracas, London would receive the equivalent of £16m worth of fuel. The plan was that London would actively promote the image of Venezuela in the UK in return for a deal that would subsidize the fuel bill of London buses, thereby relieving the Transport for London budget and freeing up funds for Livingstone to offer reduced bus fares to 250,000 low-income Londoners. The whole effort brought considerable policy disarray and confusion as the exchange was at odds with national government policy towards Venezuela and there were no constitutional rules in place to say that this kind of city-to-city exchange was permissible. However, neither were there rules in place to say that it was not, so Mayor Livingstone marched on in pursuit of his goal. The final scheme never reached fruition as Livingstone lost the 2008 election just as he was bringing the deal to a close. The new Mayor scrapped the whole project immediately. (Beall and Adam, 2017, 19)

In December 2018 the new mayor of Istanbul, Ekrem Imamoglu, visited Sarajevo, meeting various leaders of the Sarajevo canton but not his institutional counterpart, the Sarajevo mayor. This fact was interpreted by some as a diplomatic scandal. While Sarajevo mayor Abdulah Skaka linked it to specific political circumstances, critiques were formulated in relation to the fact that Skaka's party (the Party for Democratic Action) has close relationships with Turkish president Recep Tayyib Erdogan and his party, the AKP, and that the AKP candidate lost in Istanbul against Imamoglu, who at the time was also seen by some as a future competitor of Erdogan.[3] In this case international ideological links have had a significant impact on the city-to-city relationship: the misalignment between the mayor of the capital city of a country under significant foreign influence and the ruling party of the influential foreign power generated several frictions. Additional contention arose over the refusal to grant honorary citizenship of Sarajevo to Orhan Pamuk, a Turkish Nobel laureate who was critical of Erdogan, and over the stripping of the Plaque of the City of Sarajevo from Professor Ali Ladcioglu, who was allegedly close to the Gulen movement, an organization designated as terrorist by the Turkish government after the 2016 coup.

City diplomacy is by no mean limited to bilateral and multilateral city counterparts. Beyond nongovernmental counterparts such as foreign companies, universities, and NGOs, city mayors engage actively with foreign governments: prime ministers, ministers of foreign affairs, consulates, and trade offices, among others. While such activities are borderline from a legal point of view, insofar as government-to-government diplomatic relationships are in principle reserved to governments only, cities find a way to engage indirectly and "softly" with foreign governments. A case is provided by the city of Tokyo, taking advantage of its capital city position. Tokyo has highly developed city diplomacy, strongly rooted in the long-term strategy of the city, which represents a core element of the Office of the Governor for Policy Planning. The Tokyo Metropolitan Government's Basic Strategy for City Diplomacy was created in 2014. The strategy foresees a series of different initiatives in city-to-city and multilateral city diplomacy. The city is also very active in taking advantage of the international environment provided by the 150 embassies in the city. For example, ambassadors and representatives are invited to take part in an annual event organized to introduce Tokyo's policies and initiatives to them, and through this informal channel significant projects are developed.[4] Similarly, the city of Bristol in the UK signed a city-to-region agreement with the region of Guangzhou in China to support a number of foreign direct investments by Huawei in the Bristol/Bath area. Even more decisively, the mayor of Los Angeles meets foreign government–level leaders in its city diplomacy. The city of Los Angeles went as far as to sign a city-to-government agreement with the Ministry of Foreign Affairs of

Mexico to set up a bilateral commission (Mexico–Los Angeles) called MEXLA to develop cooperation on specific policy areas such as sport, food, trade, and culture. As Nina Hachigian, deputy mayor for international affairs of Los Angeles, past US ambassador to ASEAN, put it,

> I've found in my transition to municipal government that I still inter-
> act with diplomats all the time, negotiate the texts of agreements, and
> attend meetings between heads of state and my principal. The differ-
> ence is the immediacy of the results, which is gratifying, and the aim
> to deliver to the people in just a single metropolis. There is freedom in
> that focus: We can have a productive relationship with foreign coun-
> terparts even when tensions arise at the national level, and we can en-
> gage all kinds of local partners, such as diaspora communities, busi-
> nesses, nonprofits, and artists, to help us execute our initiatives. That
> being said, an urban scope is narrower and resources far fewer. (Hachi-
> gian 2019)

City-to-city cooperation often takes place with the support and intermediation of structures and networks—of an increasingly transnational
character—that are much wider and more complex than the simple bilateral
relationship between cities of the traditional form of twinning. Indeed, after
the practice of twinning successfully spread all over the world and brought
economic and social improvements, the next step towns made led to the creation of networks, which included not only cities, but other nonstate actors.
The new focus has shifted from the importance of twinning to the importance of networks and alliances. City networks have gone well beyond city-
twining achievements, as they include in the debate nonmunicipal actors as
well as representatives of the private sector. Networks are effectively giving
cities the international visibility they aspired to.

City *networks* deserve special mention among the many diverse initiatives
of city diplomacy. Networks provide a central infrastructure in city diplomacy to operate in the international system (Acuto et al. 2017; Acuto and
Rayner 2016; Agranoff 2014; Bansard, Pattberg, and Widerberg 2017; S. Barber 1997; Baycan-Levent, Gülümser Akgün, and Kundak 2010; Caponio
2018; Jayne et al. 2011; Kern and Bulkeley 2009; Lusk and Gunke 2018; Stanley 2005). In response to the inability of national governments to reach significant agreements on a global level, cities have started to look to each other
to channel in a more structured way their common stakes and ambitions and
to gain more international leverage. Within these transmunicipal platforms
cities gather, share best practices and experiences, cooperate on a voluntary

peer-to-peer basis, and build partnerships that often involve also the private sector. Over past decades, such networks have become powerful urban alliances that allow municipalities to push for change by jointly addressing a broad range of global issues, from climate change to public transportation and infrastructure, from security to health and building peace. City-to-city networks have grown in number from 55 in 1985 to over 2,015 (Acuto and Rayner 2016), and they may cover several topics, often within the same setting (multipurpose networks). Many cities are part of an international network. And yet, only 1 percent of city budgets usually goes to networking and international activities, and most often there is no specific training for managing and negotiating within city networks. Networks can be national, regional, or international/global. Among the 170 cases explored by Acuto and Morissette (Acuto et al. 2017), the state-based networks are still the majority, representing 49 percent of them; these arrangements are organized by the central state. The data show how important states continue to be in international relations: in the era of state decadence, they are still relevant as creators of city networks. Some relevant examples of national city networks include:

The *US Conference of Mayors*, which includes more than 1,400 American cities with populations of over 30,000.

The *Associazione Nazionale Comuni Italiani*, which includes as members almost all the Italian municipalities.

The *Key Cities Group* in the United Kingdom, which includes medium-sized municipalities; it coexists with other similar subnational associations of cities.

The *Association of Municipalities of the Netherlands*.

The *Association of Municipalities of Rwanda*.

Regional as well as international networks are increasing: the former comprise 21 percent of total cases, while the latter represent 29 percent. While nation-based organizations of municipalities are still diffused, at the international level city networks are thriving. Examples of regional networks of cities and local authorities include:

Eurocities. This group brings together over 130 large cities in Europe with a total population of more than 130 million people.

Council of European Municipalities and Regions. A group of other minor associations of municipalities in the wider European region.

Mercociudades. Founded in 1995, this network includes more than 353 cities from 10 countries in the MERCOSUR region. Member cities have a total population exceeding 120 million. The cities network also has close relations with MERCOSUR, the regional intergovernmental institution.

CITYNET. This aggregation includes more than 100 members from more than 20 Pacific Asia states.

Organization of Islamic Capitals and Cities. The largest association in the Arabian Peninsula; affiliated with the OIC.

Med Cities. Established in 1991, this group now brings together more than 50 local authorities from all shores of the Mediterranean basin.

International city networks are growing in number and power. Some are of long standing, others are recent. All aim to have an impact on major global issues. Significant examples include the following:

United Cities and Local Governments (UCLG). Founded in 2004, this is the biggest organization of subnational governments in the world, with more than 240,000 members from across the globe (cities and local and regional authorities). UCLG represents over half of the world's population and presents itself as the united voice of and advocate for democratic, local self-government. It has committees on such topics as decentralization, local development, culture, gender equality and social inclusion, human rights, participative democracy, urban strategic planning, mobility, and city diplomacy. In addition, the UCLG has a dedicated department for large metropolitan areas (*Metropolis*). Its activities consist mainly of transnational meetings, advocacy at the UN level, peer-to-peer training, and exchanges on urban policymaking and practices.

C40—Cities Climate Leadership Group. Launched in 2005 on an initiative of then-mayor of London Ken Livingstone, it now has more than 90 member cities, including Sydney, Johannesburg, Rio de Janeiro, Hong Kong, Milan, Rome, and Venice, and megacities such as Tokyo, Seoul, Los Angeles. and Mexico City. Overall, it represents one in twelve people worldwide as well as 25 percent of the entire world economy. The mission of C40 is to tackle climate change from below, with cities as key elements and obligatory passage points for environmental security. Network activities go beyond summits and meetings, aiming to reduce carbon dioxide emissions and advocate for substantial action from both national governments and private corporations. Currently chaired by Paris mayor Anne Hidalgo, C40 has carried out

intense lobbying in recent years—for instance, during relevant rounds
of the Conferences of Parties within the UN Framework Convention
on Climate Change held in Montreal (COP11, 2005), Copenhagen
(COP15, 2009), and Paris (COP21, 2015).

International Council for Local Environment Initiatives (ICLEI).
Founded in 1990, this group gathers local governments committed to
the cause of sustainable urban development. Its growing membership
now includes over 1,200 cities, towns, provinces, and regions from 84
countries. ICLEI's work is based on a bottom-up approach that considers locally designed initiatives as crucial, effective, and cost-efficient
means to implement national and global objectives and targets. It provides training, consulting, information, and technical support as well
as formal and informal platforms for knowledge sharing and capacity
building.

WHO Healthy Cities. Launched by the World Health Organization in
the 1980s, this project connects over 4,000 municipalities on issues
related to public health in urban areas.

Compact of Mayors. Launched in 2014 by then–secretary general of the
UN, Ban Ki-Moon, along with Michael Bloomberg, former mayor of
New York City and UN special envoy for cities and climate change. It
is a global coalition of municipal leaders united around the goal of
fighting climate change through coordinated local climate action.
Through measuring cities' impact on climate and through risk analysis, the members have agreed on local actions, such as setting targets
for reducing greenhouse gas emissions. The Compact of Mayors is
part of a common effort against climate change in joint cooperation
with the C40 Group, ICLEI, UCLG, and UN-Habitat. In 2016 it
merged with the European *Covenant of Mayors* into the new *Global
Covenant of Mayors for Climate and Energy*, which unites over 7,000
cities from 119 countries across the globe.

Mayors for Peace. Established in Japan in 1982 by then-mayor of Hiroshima, Takeshi Araki, this is a global network of cities that promotes
peace, in particular advocating for the elimination of nuclear weapons
by 2020. As of 2017, it counts more than 7,400 member cities from
around the world.

Global Parliament of Mayors. This organization was created out of the
bold proposal suggested in 2013 by the late political theorist Benjamin
Barber in his famous book *If Mayors Ruled the World*. Based in the
Hague, it was been launched in September 2016 by mayors from large
and small and developed and developing cities on all continents. Con-

vened to identify the public goods of citizens and their interests, it is a new democratic global governance body that aims to be "a global megaphone for a common urban voice and a global platform for common urban action." It works in cooperation with existing urban networks to give a more democratic basis to international policymaking and thus to forge "a planet ruled by cities."

Mega-Cities Project. A network that links the 18 major metropolitan areas in the world to encourage the exchange of ideas and technologies.

AIVP. The worldwide network of port cities, this is an interesting sectoral network that aggregates cities that are crucial nodes in global maritime activity.

Cities decide to join international networks for a variety of reasons. According to the report of the Initiative on Cities of Boston University, the primary reasons mayors join networks include the opportunity to amplify their message by uniting around common interests (32 percent), to signal to local constituents that they share a particular priority (25 percent), to exchange best practices or other information with peer cities (23 percent), and as a response to a perceived leadership vacuum on certain related issues (14 percent) (Lusk and Gunke 2018). Often, on joining international networks, mayors get socialized regarding a certain issue and compared to nonmember mayors start feeling a sense of agency to counteract policies that are considered wrong.

City networks do not only include cities; other types of actors often join them. Regions, provinces, think tanks, philanthropic foundations, and international organizations sometimes also participate. Established in 2013 by the Rockefeller Foundation in the wake of Hurricane Katrina and Superstorm Sandy, for instance, the (now defunct) *100 Resilient Cities Network* was born out of the idea that local governments need help planning for disasters and combating persistent social maladies. Similarly, *Bloomberg Philanthropies* has launched a number of different projects to enhance cities' ability to solve critical challenges by promoting public-sector innovation capacity and spreading proven and promising solutions to cities around the world. UNESCO has also partnered with more than 200 cities in the *UNESCO Creative Cities Network.*

Cities can engage in networks addressing a large list of topics; sometimes the same network works for different purposes. The first organizations properly defined as city networks (dating back to the late nineteenth century) were mostly devoted to governance and representation; their importance grew during the following decades. At first, few of them were dedicated to themes such as the environment, development, or economics. This trend reversed with the start of the new millennium; for instance, with the spread of scientific discoveries concerning human-caused climate change, cities found a new leading role, because they were the source of the greatest gas emissions. Many networks address other new topics, such as gender issues, peace building, and poverty and inequality (Acuto et al. 2017). Different internal dynamics can be observed in network politics, and overlapping themes can sometimes be an obstacle to the good functioning of the networks. The more the city participates in networks, the more its administrative structure is overloaded with demands for communications, logistics, and personnel. The cities that make the difference in city networks are generally well organized and well financed. Networks may also be influenced by the surrounding "landscape"—when several organizations have similar goals and members, the most influential, visible, and efficient will survive at the expense of the others.

Hosting global events is a further significant component of the international political projection of cities (Acuto 2013b; Andranovich, Burbank, and Heying 2001; Cochrane et al. 1996; Forcellese 2013; Giulianotti 2015; Shoval 2002). Although the organization of global events has an important economic dimension, I include this kind of activity in this section because of its public relations impact. The top three prizes in terms of generating the greatest exposure are the Olympic Games, the Federation of International Football Associations (FIFA) World Cups, and world expos. Major events can have multiple impacts on the soft power, perceptions, and international reputations of host cities. In fact, hosting such global events has an impact on development as well as perceptions of the international image and importance of the city; attributing the importance of such events only to mere economic benefits is clearly an understatement. In particular, following the worldwide success of the 1984 Summer Olympics in Los Angeles, there has been a significant increase in competition between cities to host major international events, which are seen as tools to strengthen global status in an era of growing long-distance competition. International events are so important that major cities set up quasi-independent companies to run them. This is the case of "London & Partners," which runs on average 80 events per year with £400M per year of revenue, or "Eventing Milan," which in 2016 alone ran more than 40,000 events with five million visitors, contributing €886M to Milan city GDP.

Indeed, through the visibility that an international event of this size allows, the increase in the global status of the host city can be translated into a corresponding increase in the city's capacity to influence the international agenda. In other words, organizing a successful global event can result in a greater weight in international decision-making. In addition, hosting a global event offers the possibility for organizing municipal administrations to finance the construction of large-scale infrastructure, which at the end of the event can be converted into buildings of public utility, such as housing, or be promoted as tourist attractions, as in the case of stadiums, monuments, or exhibitions. Finally, producing one of these events also implies an opportunity for host cities to fulfil other foreign policy objectives such as cultural and economic promotion, cooperation in exchanging know-how and best practices, and the organizing awareness campaigns for environmental or humanitarian issues. Given the complexity of implementing these events and the high risk of failure, it is necessary to keep in mind all the preparatory phases that they entail, from becoming candidates, negotiating, and lobbying. Collectively, all of these procedures are sometimes called a "mega-event strategy," which requires coordinated action that can include the combined efforts of mayors, local governments, public administration, and businesses. To this already considerable complexity should be added the necessary collaboration between the various substate territorial entities and the central government in a multilevel dynamic.

The case of the next world expo, to be hosted by Dubai, provides a good example in this regard. The international projection of the city is going to be boosted by the 2020 Expo event, postponed to 2021 due to the COVID-19 pandemic. While Dubai's international initiatives began only recently, the city managed to fairly quickly develop an interesting network of thirty-two sister cities. These sister cities vary in location and economic power; included are cities such as Hong Kong, Paris, Moscow, Dundee, Cheb, and Granada. On a more regional level, Dubai has relations with cities such as Teheran, Tripoli, Damascus, Beirut, and Kuwait City. It is these city partnerships, among others, that Dubai will leverage to enhance the attractiveness of the next international expo.

The Economy: Push and Pull Activities, Territorial Marketing, and City Branding

A main force that pushes a city to go international is economic interests. The economic dimension of city diplomacy is crucial, even more so now in a context of highly integrated world economy. Self-interest prevails, with cities seeking material gains mainly through activities to attract investments and to export goods. And even when other reasons exist, mayors must at least justify much of city diplomacy by arguing that they are attracting investment and creating jobs. A city pursues its economic interests in two fundamental ways: economic pull activities *attract* capital via (1) attracting tourists and visitors, (2) hosting headquarters of global institutions, corporations, or nonprofit organizations, and (3) holding big fairs, expositions, and the Olympics or other sport competitions (such as the World Cup, Formula 1 races, and regional championships). Economic push activities *export* local knowledge, goods, and services through business partnerships and best-practice agreements, often among cities with similar geographical locations, industry specializations, and experiences (for instance, cities with big ports or a long textile tradition).

Twinning projects often follow the economic driver. The case of Busan, in South Korea, provides an interesting example. As a harbor city, Busan has an intrinsic open attitude toward international trade and tourism. The relations the city has established are extremely well developed, and involve continuous ambitious projects of renovation and development, such as creating an international industrial logistics complex. Today, the city counts twenty-six sister and eleven friendship cities across the globe. Reliance on such twinning programs dates back in time; for instance, the sisterhood with Los Angeles in the US was established in 1967. The partnerships include many other cities with important harbors, such as Shanghai, Barcelona, Rio de Janeiro, and Saint Petersburg.[5]

The basic economic promotion toolkit includes promotion of inward investment, trade missions and trade shows, and tourism, as well as attracting talent. In itself, the fact that most of national GDP is created in cities does not make cities powerful actors. It takes a proactive attitude to transform this economic strength into effective power for the mayors. Directly promoting the economic structure in a foreign country is also a possible way to develop a commercial exchanges with the city; it often takes the form of dedicating specific evenings or events to the operators of the various economic sectors concerned. Verona, for example, offers the "Destination Verona" program to all countries with which it undertakes diplomatic relations. Cities undertake multiple forms of economic promotional activity, including bidding for and hosting major events such as the Olympics, investing in cultural events, having policy exchanges regarding best practices, and engaging in international networks of various kinds, as well as through urban design and architecture statements and infrastructure investment. Mayoral speeches, media articles, and the web presences and profiles of cities also play their part.

The pull economy constitutes the most common type of international actions implemented by cities, to such an extent that in more and more cases, global cities such as New York, Tokyo, and London have offices specialized in this sector (Van Der Pluijm and Melissen 2007). It is therefore interesting to note that there is a general positive trend in the professionalization of municipal public administration in activities to promote capital flows and tourism from abroad. Most of these structures are located in large cities, whose economies are often larger than those of medium-sized countries. But even smaller cities often pursue the same goals and are diplomatically committed to bringing economic benefits to their communities. In addition, various diplomatic actions are used to encourage international companies and institutions to transfer their headquarters to their territory. Examples include Frankfurt, one of the largest financial centers in the world, where the European Central Bank and Deutsche Bank are located; and, of more modest size, the Hague, global capital of international law, with courts such as the International Court of Justice, the International Criminal Court, and the International Tribunal.

Tourism has become one of the world's major trade categories, ranking fourth after fuels, chemicals, and food. Globally, cities such as London and Hong Kong remain top tourist destinations. Many European cities, such as Rome, Florence, and Milan, attract tourists because they are religious, cultural, and fashion centers. Because tourism is an important economic tool for cities, many cities have transformed their economies by deliberately promoting the city as a tourist destination. Economic promotion, tourism, and investment are very much interconnected. In some ways, one could even consider tourism and investments to be subcategories of economic promotion; both of them are sources of money and provide an incentive to improve cities' attractiveness. Nobody has exclusive control over economic promotion; both public and private institutions may practice measures that capture people or investments. Civic and cultural institutions may achieve the same result, whether they behave as local institutions' arms or as separate entities. Thus, the organic nature of cities allows many competing bodies to contribute together to improve the international profile of their city. Tourism is strongly influenced by a city's profile; many factors determine tourists' choice to visit a certain city. First, people are attracted by historical heritage, culture, and fashion, which is why Italian and French cities are among the towns visited the most. Tourists are also captured by lifestyle, social atmosphere, openness, tolerance, and livability in general. Good examples are Spanish cities (especially Barcelona and Madrid, considered the most cosmopolitan cities of Spain) and all the urban centers of northern European countries. In the end, the role played by technology and finance must not be forgotten; New York, London, and Hong Kong continue to be the most desirable cities to visit on holiday, because they can be seen as representing the highest aspirations of life: Wall Street has been the subject of movies and books, and is always cited as the heart of global wealth. However, it is remarkable that among the ten most-visited cities of the world in 2017, seven were in Asia.

Education constitutes an important element of the pull effect of cities. The value of foreign students to cities goes way beyond the fees they pay to universities and the spending they generate in the local economy. The value also lies in the long-term relationship that is built, which will shape students' lifelong affinity to that city. City diplomacy strategies increasingly focus on student recruitment, working with universities to outline the benefits not just of studying a given course, but of the total experience of living there and taking part in city life. As international students integrate into the life of the city beyond their college or university, they are likely to build shared values and long-term relationships. There has been a definite trend for both established cities and new world cities to work to attract students from emerging market cities and countries. The established cities often attract internationally mobile students by virtue of the strength of their profiles and the world-class reputations of their universities.

Great events, such as the Olympics, the World Cup, and world expos, are important and increasingly controversial. Those events undoubtedly generate great exposure for the city. Among the benefits are the improvement of sectorial businesses, major public-private cooperation related to investments and partnerships, and the expansion of tourism. Those inputs inevitably lead to development, so there is good chance that the city will profit from hosting events. The key to success seems to be aligning hosting such an events with a longer-term strategy, as with the London Olympics, which were used to foster the policy of moving the center of activity in the city to the east. Nevertheless, if inadequately managed, events may also cause a loop of indebtedness, with many side effects, including corruption and criminal infiltration. This explains way some mayors are reluctant to bid for the Olympics and other high-profile events. For example, the Olympics in Athens cost to the city a bill that citizens are still paying today.

Push-economy activities focus on improving the commercial balance and promoting the export of goods, services, and know-how in general. Cities in most cases use commercial or association agreements to support the export of local goods. While initial agreements allow the increase of commercial exchanges—that is, of goods and services—between the companies present in the territories of the two parties, a second stage of agreements establishes reciprocal exchanges of best practices or know-how. Consequently, while the first agreements concern economic goods proper—that is, goods subject to sale in accord with market dynamics—the second type relate to skills and competencies that produce no immediate economic gain but that produce common long-term benefits for the parties. A concrete example of the latter type of relationships is the multidimensional partnerships between Antwerp and Durban.

To generate benefits for their economies, cities compete with each other. As already mentioned, they do this to attract branches and operational centers of multinational companies, international organizations, and supranational institutions (as recently occurred in post-Brexit Europe with the relocation of EU agencies from the UK to continental Europe), as well as international events and sports. Competition to host major international events is an excellent example of cities' direct commitment to diplomacy as a means of benefiting their economies. The cities carry out real first-level negotiations both to increase their prestige and reputation in the world and to attract large infrastructure and development projects, which will produce effects destined to remain after the event has ended. In this case, however, the mere commitment of the city's diplomats is not enough; a wider collaboration with the other national actors is necessary.

Marketing and place branding are increasingly central in the economic promotion of city diplomacy (Kotler, Haider, and Rein 1993; Valdani and Ancarani 2000). An aspect of particular interest within pull economic activities is city branding, applying techniques of business marketing to the promotion of a city, which is advertised like any brand, as with "I Love NY" (Lucarelli and Berg 2011). Among cities attracting investments, the most successful are the new world cities, such as Amsterdam, Berlin, and Copenhagen, that have an advanced apparatus for promotion that pushed investors to bet on them. Those three cities provide examples of well-thought-out marketing campaigns that brought fame of their slogans: "I Am sterdam," "Be Berlin" and "Cop en hagen." Here the message is directed at the individual, and the point is that these cities permit you to pursue your own interests. It is evident that the image cities present to the outside world can be unconnected to that of the nation-state to which it belongs. While as a tool for marketing city branding is mostly concentrated in the economic domain to attract investments, tourism, and big events (Kavaratzis 2004; Lucarelli and Berg 2011), its political dimension is equally relevant. Branding can be turned into identity building (Kavaratzis and Ashworth 2005). It is through constructing a city narrative that the city builds up a certain public image that produces soft power and the ability to influence political processes at the national and international levels. The city of Medellín in Colombia offers an interesting example of how imaginative city leadership has transformed the image of the city internationally. Once known as home to Pablo Escobar, the notorious narcotics trafficker, it is now possible to enjoy civic spaces and consumer delights in middle-class neighborhoods and to visit the city's surrounding working-class communities by way of the city's new cable-car network. In 2013 Medellín was hailed as the "most innovative city in the world" by the influential Urban Land Institute, and in 2016, it won the Lee Kuan Yew World City Prize, awarded in recognition of innovative and sustainable urban solutions. An important part of this transformation, which has been described as nothing short of a "metropolitan miracle," was a result of the foresight of ambitious city politicians, which led to, among other things, to hosting the prestigious UN-Habitat World Economic Forum in 2014 (Beall and Adam 2017).

A strong, unique, and recognizable identity is needed in the global city competition. Urban marketing intends to generate an emotional link to the city to activate attraction and desire. The city becomes a consumer good to be sold on the market of global attractions. Success is achieved when the right narrative is broadcast globally. Storytelling becomes an important asset in city internationalization strategies. The objective is to associate the city with a specific lifestyle that cannot be adopted anywhere else. Life fulfillment, good quality of life, and once-in-a-lifetime experiences come to be exclusively associated with that specific urban context. The Grand Tour of the seventeenth and eighteenth centuries in Italy is a classic example. At that time, a months-long stay in Florence, Rome, and Venice was considered a necessary step in the individual bildung of any well-educated Westerner (Belfanti 2019). Later, desirable cities included Paris, London, and more recently, New York. The city branding of NY is particularly illustrative with its famous formula, "I Love NY," with the word "love" represented by a stylized heart. This famous symbol of New York, omnipresent on posters, stickers, T-shirts, and fridge magnets, was created in 1976, when the Department of Commerce of New York entrusted the task to the designer Milton Glaser.

Johannesburg is a good example of an emerging city that is investing to promote its international brand. In the city of Johannesburg, the External Relations Unit handles the international development of the city. The unit is divided into three sections, each fostering a specific task, from promoting twinning programs to supporting other government offices. The city logo, "Joburg, a World Class African City," is explicitly aimed at positioning the city in the international mindset by combining a global and a local component, the so-called "glocal" strategy. In this way, while Johannesburg's international strategy is intended to raise the visibility of the city, there is also a strong focus on making the city an entry point for the rest of Africa. In line with this approach, Johannesburg has various projects and partnerships with both African and non-African cities, such as a library exchange with Birmingham (England), a land and housing development project with Addis Ababa (Ethiopia), and various service-related projects with Windhoek (Namibia).[6]

The city imaginary is becoming more and more central and it is on this imaginary that city managers need to build up their branding strategies. There is an unnoticed competition between countries and cities in the global imaginary. Are we first and foremost citizens of a country or of a city? Traditionally in the last few centuries, our identity was linked to the former, but recently the latter is gaining more and more prominence. Plus, historically speaking the city identity is much more permanent than a national identity. From a long durée perspective, my Roman identity is longer lasting than my Italian identity. Is the power of attraction of New York City more or less intense than that of the United States? Is London more appealing than the UK? Is Shanghai more fascinating than China? Or, put in other terms, would the UK still be equally charming without London? Would Italy still be so enchanting without Rome? Would Greece be captivating without Athens? Even best performing series, such as "Money Heist/La casa de papel/The House of Paper," have their characters identified with names of cities: Rio, Denver, Moscow, Nairobi, Lisbon, Berlin, Stockholm. This city bonding gives an intensity that can be hardly found anywhere else.

Linked to the city branding is the wider city strategy for internationalization. Key to this is the city mayor producing a strategic document. Buenos Aires provided an interesting example in this regard. The city has a General Secretariat for International Relations (Secretaría General y Relaciones Internacionales) that coordinates the various international activities of the city. In recent years, the city has developed its first strategy for the international projection of the city. Among the objectives of the strategy is attracting visitors, students, and economic activities. The strategy is based on the recognition that Buenos Aires has what it takes to be one of the major players among global cities. The strategy includes a section on identity, reputation, and visibility; the aim is to foster the role and image of the city as a global capital and as an example of good quality of life. Culture plays an important role in the proposed image of a harmonious city. In this vein, the city is a member of UNESCO Creative Cities Network to promote creativity and creative expressions among local industries. This has initiated projects such as the Design District and Bienal Arte Joven (Young Art Biennale), which are intended as building blocks for the contemporary branding for the city. The strategy is grounded in a series of activities and objectives to be achieved by 2023.[7]

City branding and the internationalization strategy of the city are linked to the potential soft power that cities can develop (Beall and Adam 2017). Every city that has experienced a "golden age," from fifth-century BC Athens, to fifteenth-century Florence, sixteenth-century London, and nineteenth-century Vienna, has drawn in ideas, people, and commerce from as wide a circle as the technology of their day would allow. Cities have always been hives of ambition and activity, explosive expressions of culture, trade, and the economy. The more open and inviting, the more cosmopolitan a city is, the more its soft power expands and is reinforced. This remains a key challenge for the internationalization strategy of the city: finding the right balance between the political, economic, and cultural vectors of the city in such a way as to create a unique, inspiring dream. To achieve this, city managers need to be ambitious and skillful enough to bring the different forces of the urban context to work in an internationally consistent way. A push from the national brand might in some cases help (but also the opposite might be true in different circumstances), but every city has a chance to play the game of capturing the global imaginary to become a point of reference for economic and political actors, as well as for artists, students, and tourists.

Culture and Environment

A soft but important dimension for the international projection of cities is culture. Cultural diplomacy has always been one of the most important prerogatives of the role a country plays abroad, and it obviously also applies to city diplomacy. The cultural exchange that the actors promote on the international scene is an instrument of mutual knowledge that stimulates better cooperation between parties and the achievement of certain objectives. Cities originally collaborated in the cultural field through twinning. Today this frame is no longer necessary to carry out cultural diplomacy, and relations have broadened. Nowadays cultural diplomacy involves intercultural exchanges, migration networks, the presence of relevant cultural hubs (museums, galleries, theaters), the organization of big events (art exhibitions, music shows, or movie festivals), or appointment as a European Capital of Culture for a one-year period. Cities deploy museums, artists, and cultural institutions to gain cultural enrichment and reinforce their external projection.

A historical example of cultural diplomacy is the centrality, during the Cold War, of the role of ideology in the diplomatic missions of the United States toward NATO allies, aimed at strengthening and maintaining the common cultural sense of belonging to a Western bloc. US policymakers considered cultural diplomatic action to be an integral part of national security policy. The parallel involvement of cities in international sociocultural activities dates back to the same period, when the federal government in the US case, and local authorities in the European case, implemented town twinning projects across the Iron Curtain. These local initiatives were aimed at preventing the outbreak of new hostilities by promoting social and cultural exchanges.

This sociocultural aspect has gradually become the object of external actions by local governments, so much so that today it is a fundamental dimension of the growing phenomenon of city diplomacy in general. Recent city partnership agreements in fact show how the sociocultural sphere plays a leading role in many cases, even going beyond traditional twinning initiatives. The diplomatic action of cities in this area is carried out in many concrete ways, from cooperation in the creation of exhibitions, shows, and artistic performances in general to exchanges of young people for sporting events or students in educational programs, from collaboration between public hospitals or between universities and research centers to the simple organization of cultural visits for institutional representatives, and the formulation of common guidelines to promote and maintain cultural heritage. It is interesting to note that the movement of people is often the privileged tool for actions in the sociocultural field, given the necessary correlation between exchanges of individuals and exchanges of ideas; it is an essential element for any action aimed at bringing people and cultures closer together. The growing importance of this dimension in the diplomatic action of cities has been acknowledged in Agenda 21 of the Working Group on Culture of the United Cities and Local Governments, which establishes how cultural promotion should be at the center of every urban strategy.

Famous examples of cities that are heavily invested in culture come from the Gulf area. Dubai has developed a clear strategy to attract world-renowned universities to project an image of an educational hub. Similarly, Abu Dhabi has significantly invested in attracting museums, opening branches of the Guggenheim and the Louvre. In terms of networks, it is worth mentioning again the UNESCO Creative Cities Network that was created in 2004 to promote cooperation with and among cities that have identified creativity as a strategic factor for sustainable urban development. The 246 cities that currently make up this network work together toward a common objective: placing creativity and cultural industries at the heart of their development plans at the local level and cooperating actively at the international level. It is yet another example of hybrid networking in which international institutions and cities from all continents work together to promote culture transnationally in urban contexts.

Environmental protection represents one of the areas of greatest difficulty in coordination between the different city diplomacy actions, but at the same time it is an area with the highest growth in participation by local authorities (Betsill and Bulkeley 2004; Bulkeley and Schroeder 2009; Castán Broto 2017; Kern and Bulkeley 2009; Reckien et al. 2018; Setzer 2015). Although this goal traditionally received little attention among the main fields of activity of diplomacy, it is today a topic of growing importance at an international level. Global warming has a clear local dimension. With reference to the growing activity of cities in this area, it is important to note that local governments, given the process already illustrated of the devolution of powers by the state, are increasingly endowed with authority over key sectors, such as land management, waste disposal, urban mobility, and energy consumption (Betsill and Bulkeley 2004). Therefore, the purely local dimension of environmental problems and the growing competence of cities to at least limit ecological degradation lead cities to play an ever-greater role in the field. Furthermore, it is interesting to note that sometimes the intervention of local authorities on this issue takes place collectively, through transnational networks and international associations of cities and local authorities, which are often mobilized in reaction to the ineffectiveness or disinterest of the respective national governments. Examples of such activities are those offered by the International Council for Environmental Initiatives, Cities for Climate Protection, and the Clinton Climate Initiative.

It is also important to remember the close relationship between the various relevant UN agencies and local authorities, as prominently evidenced by the cooperation agreement signed between UN-Habitat and United Cities and Local Governments in 2004 (Gutierrez-Camps 2013). The actions of these international associations have a dual purpose: to collectively develop local policies that are environmentally sustainable, and to influence and push their respective national governments to create greater awareness worldwide climate issues in the international community. The relationship established in this way between local authorities and states once again shows that the national government has a strong influence on the city's foreign policy objectives, and that multilevel actions are growing progressively stronger within the global governance system, configuring the city as an institution active in the diplomatic sphere.

The Paris Agreement has recognized the role of local and regional authorities in addressing climate change. At the Conference of the Parties (COP21) in Paris, on 12 December 2015, parties to the United Nations Framework

Convention on Climate Change (UNFCCC) reached a landmark agreement to combat climate change and to accelerate and intensify the actions and investments needed for a sustainable low-carbon future. The agreement recognizes the role of nonparty stakeholders in addressing climate change, including cities, other subnational authorities, civil society, and the private sector. They were invited to scale up their efforts and support actions to reduce emissions, build resilience and decrease vulnerability to the adverse effects of climate change, and to uphold and promote regional and international cooperation. In this context, a number of cities and regions decided to step up their actions to reduce emissions regardless of, and at times in tension with, their respective national positions, showing once again a certain degree of growing international agency.

Especially on environmental issues, cities at times engage directly with international institutions, bypassing their national government. A case in point is New York City, which was one of the first cities to submit a Voluntary Local Review (VLR) directly to the United Nations reporting on the progress toward sustainable development goals. Modeled after the Voluntary National Review that countries are invited to submit to the High-Level Political Forum every year, the VLR highlights the city's sustainable development achievements. When adopting the 2030 Agenda, United Nations member states committed to working closely with local and regional governments to implement the sustainable development goals (SDGs). Since 2015, metropolises, small cities, regions, and their associations alike have been actively localizing the 2030 Agenda, bringing sustainable development goals closer to the people they serve and using the framework as a tool for planning and execution. As part of its follow-up and review mechanisms, the 2030 Agenda for Sustainable Development encourages member states to "conduct regular and inclusive reviews of progress at the national and sub-national levels, which are country-led and country-driven" (par. 79). Par. 89 of the 2030 Agenda calls on major groups and other stakeholders, including local authorities, to report on their contribution to the implementation of the agenda. In this spirit, local and regional governments are increasingly engaging in such subnational reviews of the implementation of sustainable development goals via the VLRs. VLRs use the common language of the global goals to translate local actions to a global audience. It is a format that is accessible to the UN community as well as other stakeholders following the SDG process, in line with United Nations Economic and Social Council documents recognizing the key role of local governments in implementing sustainable development goals. While VLRs have no official status, the process of undertaking these subnational reviews provides multiple benefits to the entities engaging in them and to implementing sustainable development. In this way, the VLR gives local governments of all sizes a concrete tool to become directly involved with the work of the United Nations for the first time. VLRs can also help reinforce vertical coherence and complement and contribute to the national Voluntary National Reviews of sustainable development implementation. As of today, more than twenty cities are engaged directly with the UN.[8]

Security: From Conflicts to COVID

The potential for cities to be cradles of global peace is clear and powerful precisely because historically, cities have been the single greatest sources of atrocity, war, and violent nationalistic, colonial, and religious antipathies. The great Nazi rallies were held in Nuremberg or Berlin rather than the Black Forest; Mussolini marched on Rome, not the Cinque Terre; the 1917 Russian Revolution was centered in Moscow, and the Terror of the French Revolution in Paris. The city-states of ancient Greece and Renaissance Italy waged continual war with one another; the Punic Wars began and ended in Rome and Carthage. The Thirty Years' War began with the Defenestration of Prague, and its greatest atrocity was the sack and burning of Magdeburg. All of this atrocity and destruction originated and was executed in cities. It is precisely by looking at these and other examples that we can understand the tremendous potential of cities as powerful, unprecedented sources of global peace.

An important field of operation of city diplomacy is peace and security. From urban peacebuilding (Björkdahl 2013; Routledge 2010) to urban insecurity (Ashworth 1991; Graham 2010; Rodrigues, Brancoli, and Amar 2017) and peace-building initiatives in war zones (Gartung 2000; Van Der Pluijm and Melissen 2007), cities have been intensely active on peace and security (Desch 2001; Graham 2010; Musch 2008; Stanley 2003). In recent years, actors other than national states have committed themselves to assisting the populations and institutional structures of countries that have found themselves in armed conflicts. Nongovernmental organizations, civil society associations, and religious groups also have great influence in these situations. Cities have carved out an important role in this area because often the roots and consequences of conflicts are local. For this reason, having an interlocutor such as a city that understands local needs is often crucial. An added value that is rarely present in the case of states is that cities are generally perceived as neutral actors and honest brokers, thanks to the fact that they do not possess weapons. Especially at the end of World War II, city-to-city interactions constituted a prime example of aid for postwar reconstruction or assistance in situations of conflict through town twinning projects. Today cities promote peace and the growth of their counterparts through helping to develop good local governance. Evidence of the evolution of the security dimension of city diplomacy can be found in the new approaches used by cities in conflict areas, methods that have now diverged from the old town twinning. The UCGL has established a "Taskforce for Crisis Prevention and Management."

Since the end of the Cold War, with the transition from the balance-of-power bipolar system to the current one characterized by multiple actors and dynamics, new wars have become more frequent. The emergence of new conflicts and new actors involved in them has been accompanied by expanded participation in resolving the conflicts themselves, with new actors equipped with many new diplomatic tools. In this context, we are witnessing progressive participation in conflict resolution and prevention, mediation and peace building, by local governments and cities (Stanley 2003). In this regard, Van der Pluijm focuses on the reasons why the security dimension has begun to take a leading role in city diplomacy. First, given that the primary causes of the outbreak of a conflict, as well as the victims mainly affected in its development, are both local, cities appear to be the most suitable political entities to provide their expertise. Furthermore, despite the ongoing process of devolution of powers from central to local governments, the state remains the exclusive jurisdiction of military defense of the territory. As a result, cities are unarmed political entities, and for this reason are less likely to perceive conflicts as problems of a military nature only. It is for this reason that, in their international actions in war areas, cities use different means than the military ones typical of the state. Finally, cities that are less connected to the international community than states will tend to express themselves less in a single voice and therefore constitute a diverse plurality of potential interlocutors for the actors involved in the conflict. For all these reasons, cities are perceived to be closer to the local reality of new conflicts, and the parties involved in the conflicts perceive them as more neutral (Van Der Pluijm and Melissen 2007).

From a historical point of view, it is interesting to note how the involvement of local authorities in security matters can be traced back to the colonial era, when the British Empire was among the first to promote local participation, encouraging local Indian community involvement as a way to prevent riots. This is one of the original cases that led to the perception of local communities as sources not only of conflict, but of peacekeeping. However, it was only after World War II that city-to-city cooperation programs developed in the field of security. In this regard, recall the already-mentioned twinning initiatives of the cities of Western Europe and the United States with the cities of Eastern Europe across the Iron Curtain. Contemporary city diplomacy, however, involves actions more and more distant from the simple twinning of the 1950s; the operations undertaken have become progressively more specialized and professionalized. In fact, with the gradual recognition by the international community of a positive correlation between security and development, promoting efficient local governance is seen to a greater extent as a valid tool for conflict resolution and peacekeeping. Thus, in the field of international security we are witnessing a diversification of roles between the state and the city. While the state is increasingly limited to financing programs, cities mainly play the practical role of implementing the aforementioned programs.

In conflict-related activities, cities can decide to intervene in three distinct moments: before, during, and after the outbreak of a war. When the commitment occurs before the start of the violence, there is talk of preventive actions to avoid aggravating the current situation. Historically, city activism of this type has in many cases had only limited results. A main example of this is the Mayors for Peace initiative, established in 1982 by the mayor of Hiroshima, with the aim of preventing future nuclear attacks, bringing the attention of the international community to the abolition of nuclear weapons. Another is the Rwandese Association of Local Government Authorities (RALGA), who was funded by the International Cooperation Agency of the Association of Netherlands Municipalities in order to, in part, prevent new crimes against humanity in the postgenocide Rwandan situation; it also helped reduce poverty, improve the decentralization of the political system, and encourage collaboration in achieving good local governance to prevent new ethnic tensions in the future. Other interesting cases are the mobilization of American cities against the war in Iraq, and the Congress of Mayors of the Capitals of the World sponsored by the Florentine mayor Giorgio la Pira in the 1950s to stop nuclear escalation. At times, activism has generated significant results: the intervention of the Association of Dutch Municipalities in Rwanda was positive, leading to the creation of the Rwandan Association of Local Governments.

However, city activism may also fuel international tension, promoting an agenda that leads to political escalation, beyond central governmental action (Marchetti and Tocci 2009). An illuminating example is provided by the city of Tokyo in relation to the Senkaku/Diaoyu Islands dispute in the East China Sea. The islands were at the center of an international controversy over their sovereignty. In April 2012, former Tokyo governor Ishihara announced that the Tokyo Metropolitan Government would purchase three of the Senkaku Islands from a private owner, the Kurihara family. Donations of approximately JPY 1.4 billion (approx. $13 million USD) were collected from residents of Tokyo and other places throughout Japan. On September 2, 2012, the Tokyo Metropolitan Government conducted a field investigation of the Senkaku Islands from the sea. The purpose was to conduct a basic investigation to perform a real estate evaluation and consider measures for utilizing them. Reactions from the People's Republic of China were immediate and large-scale. The situation was regarded as "the most serious for Sino-Japanese relations in the post-war period in terms of the risk of militarized conflict."[9] Following these events, the Japanese government felt pressured to engage with the issue, and on September 11, 2012, the Senkaku Islands came to be owned by the national government. The Tokyo Metropolitan Government established a fund to prompt the national government to utilize the islands, and to strictly manage donations to keep up pressure on the dispute.

Cities can also take diplomatic actions to resolve conflicts that still continue. An example is the involvement of various European and Canadian municipalities in the Israeli-Palestinian conflict through mediation and monitoring works. Another is the twinning between different US cities, such as Denver, Dallas, and Philadelphia, with Iraqi cities such as Baghdad, Kirkuk, and Mosul, respectively. Intervention during a conflict can be undertaken in place of national diplomacy if the country concerned is not recognized internationally. Cities engage during a conflict to try to alleviate the suffering of the populations involved, as in the Italian case of the Italian Center for Peace in the Middle East, composed of representatives of local authorities, that intervenes directly in the field to provide help on technical issues such as water treatment. Another current example is the Libyan mayors from across the country working together (with financial and political support from the European Commission) under the Nicosia Initiative. This effort provides services for citizens but also political assistance, breaking the isolation of the country by developing new cooperation with European cities and regions, and contributing to state-building by paving the way for national unity bodies within the country by attempting to set up a national association of municipalities.

The final phase of intervention is the one that takes shape when a war ends. In this category, projects aimed at developing local democratic structures are particularly relevant; examples include the conferences promoted by Dutch municipalities to support the administration of the Bosnian city of Fojnica and the cooperation works of many Canadian cities in the Philippines. In these cases, it is important to understand what the war represented for the populations who suffered from it, and to try to involve them in the most appropriate way. Intervention activities can be divided into three types. First, lobbying remains central; it is intended as an engagement policy and encompasses a wide range of activities, such as campaigns alerting the public to the plight of the inhabitants and expressing solidarity and moral support. A second group of activities concerns humanitarian campaigns such as projects to improve a community planning process or a municipal service in support of the peace-building and reconstruction process. Another group of activities emphasizes dialogue aimed at reestablishing trust and a nonviolent mode of conflict resolution, and of course strengthening social cohesion in the conflict area. They can take various forms, such as negotiation and mediation, but also sports and cultural activities. Diplomatic activities take place on two levels: international (mainly activities of dialogue and lobbying through networks) and local (which can make use of all three groups of actions).

Significant in this regard is the Hague Agenda on City Diplomacy (United Cities and Local Governments 2008), which stresses that the role of local governments in conflict scenarios has been insufficiently recognized, for both its positive and negative contributions, and reaffirms that city diplomacy can help prevent and resolve violent conflicts if properly activated. Policies to prevent conflict and promote interventions for peace should appreciate the crucial positions and choices of local governments in this field. Concrete actions the UCLG recommends include sharing best practices, better training of civil staff, enhancing cooperation with civil society organizations, and better engagement with international donors and national and international institutions, including the Congress of Local and Regional Authorities of the Council of Europe, the Committee of the Regions of the European Union, the UN Peace Building Commission, the UN Department of Political Affairs, the UNDP Bureau for Crisis Prevention and Recovery, and the Fragile and Conflict-Affected Countries Group of the World Bank.

City cooperation on security can involve issues larger than conflicts. A recent focus has been violence and terrorism. A number of cities, in collaboration with national security agencies, have developed a degree of cooperation, such as the Strong Cities Network against violent extremism launched in 2015. Another interesting case concerns the activism of cities in the market for weapons. In 2016, Cambridge (US) mayor Denise Simmons decided to divest her city pension fund from nuclear weapons production, effectively removing US$1 billion from investment. These kinds of boycotts are growing. Another controversial case is the boycott, disinvest, and sanction campaign on the Israeli/Palestinian case, which was joined by dozens of cities in

Ireland, Norway, Spain, Sweden, France, the UK, Italy, Belgium, and Australia. This created a significant international controversy with Israel, and in some cases also tension with their own national governments, as in the UK, where Prime Minister Boris Johnson is planning to ban local councils from joining the boycotts, just as Margaret Thatcher did in 1988 regarding city boycotts against apartheid in South Africa.

More recently, in response to the COVID crisis, city activism in health safety has developed significantly. Cities are creating common platforms, sharing experiences, and proposing common policies to tackle COVID more effectively from below (Hachigian and Pipa 2020; Rudakowska and Simon 2020). C40 launched an economic recovery task force (C40 Cities, 2020). The Organisation for Economic Co-operation and Development (OECD) provided significant studies and analysis on the cities' response to the COVID crisis (OECD 2020). #Cities4GlobalHealth managed to collect good practices through an initiative co-led by the World Association of the Major Metropolises, United Cities and Local Governments, and the Euro–Latin American Alliance for Cooperation between Cities. Another good example is the WHO European Healthy Cities Network. It is a platform for sharing experiences and lessons learned, promoting solidarity, and coordinating support in cities across the region. It is also a vehicle for supporting the city-level implementation of guidance from the WHO and national authorities, as well as regional and national response plans, such as the WHO Strategic Preparedness and Response Plan and country preparedness and response plans.

A final line of broadly security-related activities of city diplomacy concerns the digital transformation of society. It is plain that most big data collection takes place in urban contexts. From smart cities who need to collect data about citizens' mobility and utilities consumption, to crime prevention that is increasingly using CCTV and facial recognition to tackle societal threats. In 2021 we are going to have more than 1 billion surveillance cameras, a single CCTV camera per every eight humans on Earth, with countries like China and the United States with one camera per 4.1 and 4.6 people respectively.[10] Security policies are becoming increasingly pervasive and cities remain the key theater of operation. This is ambivalently interpreted. Some consider this as a way to optimize society. Others see this as a path to social control. Cities are reacting and coalescing to share best practices and develop cooperative solutions. Interesting in this regard is the example of the Cities for Digital Rights launched in 2018 by New York City, Amsterdam, and Barcelona to promote, protect, and uphold human rights on the internet at the local and global level.[11]

Human Rights, Migration, and Development

The focus of city diplomacy on human rights is growing. Although a formal legal framework for cities and local authorities is still absent, the participation of these actors in promoting and protecting fundamental rights has increased significantly in recent decades. It is often local territorial authorities who must ensure effective compliance with human rights. It is local authorities who provide for essential public services such as health services, vocational education and training, access to drinking water, social and security assistance for vulnerable citizens, and the securing of a healthy environment. Human rights, too, has a local character, which suggests that local authorities should be legally recognized as internationally responsible bodies and be politically involved in promoting an effective guarantee of human rights. The growing recognition by the international community of the correlation between the urbanization process and many of the problems of the new millennium that limit the effective respect for human rights, and of the relevance of the city in managing these problems, is reflected by the 2030 Agenda for Sustainable Development, adopted in the UN; it establishes a global commitment to make cities and human settlements inclusive, safe, flexible, and sustainable. But the nexus of cities and human rights is not just an internal issue, it is also relevant to the external actions of the cities.

Protection of human rights is increasingly seen as a city foreign involvement goal, and actions are taken to pursue this objective (Mazzucchelli 2011). An example is Barcelona—a leading city for guaranteeing human rights, to the point of establishing a Non-Discrimination Office aimed at implementing European antidiscrimination policies within its borders. San Francisco is on the forefront of fights for gender equality, using the Convention for the Elimination of All Forms of Discrimination Against Women as the basis for its many policies. Equally significant is the commitment of certain cities, such as Amsterdam, in supporting LGBT rights abroad; it made a famous lobbying effort for Riga to allow the Gay Parade in 2006. As aforementioned, New York City, Amsterdam, and Barcelona launched the Cities Coalition for #DigitalRights, in which cities for the first time came together to protect digital rights such as privacy, data sovereignty, information self-determination, participatory democracy, and universal access to the internet on both local and global levels. Los Angeles's Mayor Garcetti raised human rights concerns in his meeting with Vietnam's prime minister Nguyen Xuan Phuc (Hachigian 2019). With the growing participation of cities in promoting and protecting human rights, the label "human rights city" has been given to the most diplomatically active municipalities in this regard (Oomen, Davis, and

Grigolo 2016; J. Smith 2017). The term "human rights city" indicates both a local community and a sociopolitical process in a local context in which human rights play a primary role as fundamental values and guiding principles, as reaffirmed by the World Human Rights City Forum in 2011. In terms of networking, an interesting case of city activism on human rights is provided by "Cities for Life—Cities Against the Death Penalty," an initiative promoted by the Italian catholic NGO community of Saint'Egidio, which for several decades has been engaged on the issue of death penalty.

Berlin is a member of this network. The Berlin city council gives great importance to its international dimension; in Berlin Town Hall, much attention is given to the seventeen partnerships and fourteen city networks it is a member of, and also to the assistance it gives to the various embassies and foreign missions on its territory. Over the years, Berlin has taken part in many international activities, ranging from international campaigns on human rights to bilateral thematic exchanges such as the "German-Chinese Exchange for Cultural Management," in which five German and five Chinese cultural managers were selected to take part in various formative activities in both Germany and China.[12]

A specific aspect of the contemporary notion of being a human rights city is the focus on migration. In an increasingly interconnected international system characterized by the liberalization of movements of goods, services, and knowledge, the issue of migratory flows, which have been increasing in recent years, has acquired a prominent role on the international agenda. As a crucial center of the intricate system that connects individuals across the planet, it is not surprising that the city has placed migration on its foreign policy agenda. Migrants represent ever-larger portions of the urban population in different areas of the world, and the impact of this phenomenon both internationally and locally is impossible to ignore. Several statistical studies prove useful in understanding the dimensions of this phenomenon. First, metropolises with over one million inhabitants are the most common destinations for migratory flows. These cities, defined as immigrant gateway cities, collectively have over forty million foreign residents, 17 percent of foreign residents worldwide (Price and Benton-Short 2008). This means that about a fifth of the migrants in the world live in one of these cities. This gives an idea of the growth of this phenomenon and indicates why it should be placed on the international agenda and managed through combined efforts of both local and central governments.

Migration concerns incoming migrants to the city as well as city diasporas abroad. These two-way movements provide a strong basis for developing intercity cooperation to manage common problems and to enjoy common opportunities. From security to business, migration affects many spheres of activity. In these circumstances, the push for action often comes from below, from the migrants themselves who can mobilize resources to induce city administrations to take action. In fact, at times the migrants themselves handle the interactions and develop projects. In both directions, the diaspora-homeland relationships constitute an important driver of city diplomacy.

A clear trend can be observed in the implementation of multilevel political strategies aimed at social inclusion of migrants and minorities. In particular, various municipal institutions create contacts with their foreign minorities by learning to use the minority language, by using multimedia means of communication, and by establishing close relationships with their respective community-based organizations. In addition, the city administration must be able to learn about its migrant population by collecting statistical data and developing indicators to measure levels of social and economic inclusion. Local leaders often make including migrants a priority within their policies, through developing assemblies or consultative committees, creating lines of contact with community-based associations, ensuring effective exposure of the local government to issues related to minorities, and politically promoting and legally simplifying naturalization procedures. Such policies constitute positive reactions by some immigrant gateways to the progressive demographic change in their local populations to manage any destabilizing impacts.

Migrations flows to the cities bring several benefits. While many municipalities, especially in the West, have declining populations, recording decreases in birth rate and corresponding increases in mortality rate, migratory inflows can compensate for their demographic decline. Furthermore, from an economic point of view, if on one hand migration simply involves a greater workforce, on the other hand it implies greater demand for services, particularly in the real estate market. In addition, the greater sociocultural diversity that immigration necessarily entails is positively correlated with entrepreneurial stimulus. The combination of these positive factors in a given community helps explain cities' growing interest in and implementation of public policies aimed at promoting the inclusion of migrants.

Furthermore, it is important to underline how the growing participation of cities on the migration issue is linked to the inactivity or ineffectiveness of central governments on this issue, and also to the strongly local dimension of the issue, which has consequences mainly for local authorities (Bendel and Stürner 2019). Recently, political tensions have arisen between national governments and city authorities on the issue of migration. In the US, several cities declared themselves as "sanctuaries," suggesting that undocumented migrants were welcome. In Europe, several cities set up welcoming policies, to the point of announcing the opening of a legal file charging EU institutions with genocide, as the mayor of Palermo, Sicily, did. Another interesting example is from Barcelona mayor Ada Colau, who went on a "diplomatic visit" to Italy to defend the Catalan NGO Open Arms, which was accused by the Italian court of criminal activities in 2018.

Some cities are international by nature, with a large foreign-born population. Zurich, for instance, has more than 30 percent foreign inhabitants, higher than the European average. The city is a member of various city networks and is committed to fostering sustainable development with its twin cities Kunming and San Francisco. Zurich has also been involved in various individual international projects, such as the Comptoir Suisse 2009 and the Shanghai 2010 Expo, in which Zurich (together with Basel and Geneva) presented various case studies, sharing know-how and building networks to contribute to global sustainable development.[13]

Development is the third link in the nexus of human rights, migration, and development. Humanitarian and emergency aid operations have historically been the first area of international activity for cities and local authorities. In fact, although initially it was civil society that played the main—if not exclusive—role in this sector, starting from the 1950s with the spread of twinning initiatives in Europe and North America in particular, municipal authorities have increasingly been involved in transnational development assistance programs. Since the end of World War II, many Western cities, driven by idealistic reasons for international solidarity, have engaged in the cooperative development activities in economically disadvantaged countries, most often through twinning projects. Unlike states, cities tend to be more effective at the local level, because it is at this level that they are more specialized. Experience suggests that top-down initiatives do not lead to the best results, so it is necessary to consider aid interventions that originate from below to produce higher-quality development.

There are two main operational areas of city diplomacy on development: assistance for humanitarian development and assistance in the event of emergencies. Humanitarian assistance entails interventions for long-lasting crises, while emergency assistance tries to buffer sudden crises. The first form of aid is expressed in the form of international loans, cash donations, and building infrastructure for social purposes, such as schools, hospitals, or water plants. Best practices or technologies may be shared, administrative structures strengthened, and democracy promoted through the development of better local governance.

The second form of assistance occurs when an emergency such as an earthquake or tsunami occurs and consists of cash donations and first assistance to the victims of the disaster. Development assistance is achieved through direct contacts between the mayors of the cities involved, city networks, or associations of the civil service and citizens' organizations that manage contacts with other operators on behalf of the municipality (Ted Hewitt 1999). Beyond the traditional twinning initiatives, cities are increasingly looking for new welfare channels, and the variety of tools used in the field is diversifying. These kinds of activities are at times carried out by municipal civil servants abroad, who on behalf of their municipality supervise projects in developing countries or in crisis areas, just as diplomats would do in an embassy.

While in the past development assistance was mainly identified with town twinning projects, today city networks are the main players in the field. The most famous is the Millennium Towns and Cities Campaign, with which affiliated cities from all over the world support the achievement of the Millennium Development Goals, which later turned into Sustainable Development Goals. The diplomatic activities employed in this case include both simple expressions of solidarity and more concrete actions such as the mobilization of resources, actively supporting civil society organizations, and lobbying central governments. Coordination between the diplomatic actions of states and cities is necessary to ensure a common external policy in development assistance. However, this can be difficult, because cities usually do not have a bureaucratic apparatus like that of central governments, so their work is less efficient and more dispersed.

Concrete examples of humanitarian aid can be long-lasting donor-beneficiary relationships such as those established by different cities in the United States with local communities in Lesotho, Benin, and Cameroon; in Australia with East Timor and Sri Lanka; and in Canada with Brazil (Van Der Pluijm and Melissen 2007). With regard to emergency development assistance, examples include the assistance operations of the international community aimed at the populations of the Iranian city of Bam after the 2003 earthquake, Southeast Asia after the tsunami in 2004, or Pakistan after the 2005 earthquake.

Part III • For the Future

Concluding Remarks on Cities in the Twenty-First Century

We are living in the century of cities. For a long time, cities have been seen as in decline, yet recent decades show us that cities are growing and their international influence is increasing. More and more, cities are crucial places for the concentration of human, financial, technological, and cultural resources. Hence, they are the most suitable places to tackle the challenging issues of the future. As UN-Habitat president Joan Clos pointed out, the problems of the cities are the problems of mankind. That's why we need a new urban agenda to empower cities to deal with global problems locally and local problems globally.

Cities are emerging on the world stage as promising new actors able to address global challenges and even to build their own foreign policy. International affairs are increasingly pluralist, and among the many NSAs today, cities definitely are increasing their relevance. Cities play a remarkable role in world affairs. They are the critical engines of the global economy thanks to their infrastructural power; they host over half of the world's population and will continue to grow in the coming decades; they allow the production and exchange of new ideas, knowledge, and political and sociocultural trends; they are free from the sovereignty burdens that usually constrain the actions of nation-states; and with their pragmatic style of governance they enjoy more trust and appreciation from citizens. Through their participation in transnational networks, cities are both socialized regarding global issues and equipped to deal with them in a more effective way. In many regards, cities seem to hold solutions. But to fully take advantage of cities' potential to address global issues, we need to assess their value and facilitate their actions. In sum, we need to be much better at studying and performing city diplomacy.

City diplomacy has become widespread among municipalities, including small, medium, and big cities from both developed and developing regions across the globe. Urban "ambassadors" have been taking this new job seriously, aware of the growing worldwide influence of cities and the need to participate more in global policymaking processes. Cities go global by connecting, attracting, exporting, pursuing their own interests, interacting, lobbying, and sharing practices. As I have shown, city diplomacy involves many different vectors, including the economic one, but reducing it to the business dimension misses much of what is taking place in city diplomacy. Cities often move independently in the international setting, complementing national foreign policies (hence the notion of "paradiplomacy"). Thanks to their "glocal" nature, cities have gained more and more centrality on the global stage compared to traditional state actors. They can design and provide local solutions, on the ground, to threats and issues that are now global, crossing borders without needing a "passport." With their local responses to global pressures, cities aim at affect global governance through policies influencing daily urban life. They are local enough to produce tangible outcomes to the issues at hand, and do so under popular control, yet they are global enough to cooperate and bring about worldwide change.

City diplomacy connects local citizens to global affairs, thereby overcoming democratic deficits. City diplomacy should then be seen as an institutional platform that allows cities to connect the global and local dimensions. In this sense, city diplomacy enhances participation, ownership, and commitment at the local level by citizens and politicians alike as they work to address concrete, global threats and common well-being and resilience. As instances of "glocal" governance, cities are public entities close to the people, but also actors engaged in global affairs: they therefore have the opportunity to influence international politics from the bottom up when nation-states are unable or unwilling to reach consensus and provide solutions. Moreover, by embracing city diplomacy and transcending the traditional state-centric model of global governance, cities offer an innovative version of cosmopolitan democracy, one that is more realistic than a world government, yet based on such fundamental features of democracy as equal participation and popular accountability.

There are risks and opportunities in the international action of cities. Taking into account that the international empowerment of cities requires significant amounts of time and resources and that the normative framework still significantly constrains the international actions of cities, a number of policy recommendations can be made to minimize risks and maximize opportunities for cities' engagement in global affairs.

- *Better internal institutional design:* setting up a clear institutional process to design, implement, and monitor "municipal foreign policy"—a long-term, coherent strategy that defines the international role of the city (purposes, actors, tools, contents, and partners). A "city diplomacy" office should be established, with professional, specialized civil servants and the additional support of external advisors, think tanks, and other relevant urban actors from diverse fields such as business, education and culture, and civil society.
- *Better societal awareness:* educating society to recognize the added value of city international engagement.
- *Better coordination with national governments:* adjusting the civic institutional structure to sustain permanent contacts with national diplomacy. Coordinating and collaborating with other levels of government (the central state, regions, and provinces) to avoid institutional competition and overlapping.
- *Better coordination with other international actors:* searching for enhanced cooperation with international organizations, multinational corporations, international nongovernmental organizations, global media broadcasts, think tanks, and other groups.
- *Better coordination with urban counterparts:* getting involved in bilateral and especially multilateral initiatives in the form of city networks.

As put by David Miller, the former mayor of Toronto: "Cities are where change is happening the fastest and we must seize the opportunities we have been presented with to make that change significant and permanent." Cities have a chance. It is up to them.

Notes

Setting the Stage

1. Data presented in 2020 at the United Nations-Habitat's Tenth World Urban Forum. https://nextcity.org/daily/entry/there-are-10000-cities-on-planet-earth-half-didnt-exist-40-years-ago

Chapter 3

1. People to People International (PTPI), established by President Eisenhower in 1956 in the United States Information Agency, aims to promote the exchange of ideas and experiences between communities and reduce the probability of new conflicts through town twinning.
2. See https://www.ibb.istanbul/en/News/Detail/1229
3. http://www.chinadaily.com.cn/global/2019-04-26/content_37462677.htm
4. https://www.theguardian.com/world/2018/oct/04/osaka-drops-san-francisco-as-sister-city-over-comfort-women-statue
5. http://edition.cnn.com/2017/06/01/us/trump-climate-deal-cities-states-defying/index.html

Chapter 4

1. https://hongkongfp.com/2020/04/24/gothenburg-axes-twin-city-agreement-with-shanghai-as-sweden-closes-all-confucius-institutes/
2. See https://www.comune.modena.it/europa/info/informazioni
3. See http://ba.n1info.com/English/NEWS/a400783/Istanbulrl
4. See https://www.seisakukikaku.metro.tokyo.lg.jp/en/
5. See https://english.busan.go.kr/SisterCities
6. See https://www.joburg.org.za/about_/Pages/About%20the%20City/About%20Joburg/International-Relations.aspx
7. See https://baglobal.buenosaires.gob.ar/item/-estrategia-de-proyeccion-internac

ional-baglobal-2cb6d631578569729f5d0c6fd2eea10b.pdf and https://www.buenosair es.gob.ar/jefedegobierno/secretariageneral/institucional-secretaria-general

8. See https://sdgs.un.org/topics/voluntary-local-reviews

9. See BBC "Viewpoints: How serious are China-Japan tensions?" https://www.bbc .com/news/world-asia-21290349

10. See https://surfshark.com/surveillance-cities

11. See https://citiesfordigitalrights.org/

12. See https://www.berlin.de/rbmskzl/en/international-relations/ and https:// www.berlin.de/rbmskzl/en/international-relations/retrospective/

13. See https://www.stadt-zuerich.ch/portal/en/index /portraet_der_stadt_zuerich/integration_and_internationalnetworks.html and https://www.stadt-zuerich.ch/prd/de/index/ueber_das_departement/medien/medien mitteilungen/2009/september/090917a.html and https:// www.stadt-zuerich.ch/prd/en/index/stadtentwicklung/aussenbeziehungen/zurich-umbrella-brand/zurich-at-the-world-expo/world-expo-2010-in-shanghai.html

References

Abu-Lughod, J. L. 1989. *Before European Hegemony: The World System, AD 1250–1350.* Oxford: Oxford University Press.

Acuto, M. 2010. "Global Cities: Gorillas in Our Midst." *Alternatives* 35(4), 425–48.

Acuto, M. 2013a. *Global Cities, Governance and Diplomacy: The Urban Link.* London: Routledge.

Acuto, M. 2013b. "World Politics by Other Means? London, City Diplomacy and the Olympics." *The Hague Journal of Diplomacy* 8(3–4), 287–311.

Acuto, M., M. Morissette, and A. Tsouros. 2017. "City Diplomacy: Towards More Strategic Networking? Learning with WHO Healthy Cities." *Global Policy* 8(1), 14–22. https://doi.org/10.1111/1758-5899.12382

Acuto, M., and S. Rayner. 2016. "City Networks: Breaking Gridlocks or Forging (New) Lock-Ins?" *International Affairs* 92(5), 1147–66. https://doi.org/10.1111/1468-2346.12700

Agranoff, R. 2014. "Local Governments in Multilevel Systems: Emergent Public Administration Challenges." *American Review of Public Administration* 44 (4 suppl.), 47S–62S. https://doi.org/10.1177/0275074013497629

Aldecoa, F., and M. Keating. 1999. "Paradiplomacy in Action: The Foreign Relations of Subnational Governments." In J. Loughlin (ed.), *Cass Series in Regional and Federal Studies.* London: Routledge.

Alger, C. F. 1990. "The World Relations of Cities: Closing the Gap between Social Science Paradigms and Everyday Human Experience." *International Studies Quarterly* 34(4), 493–518. https://doi.org/10.2307/2600609

Alger, C. F. 2010. "Expanding Governmental Diversity in Global Governance: Parliamentarians of States and Local Governments." *Global Governance* 16(1), 59–79.

Alger, C. F. 2014. *The UN System and Cities in Global Governance.* London: Springer.

Amen, M. 2011. *Cities and Global Governance: New Sites for International Relations.* Farnham: Ashgate.

Amen, M., N. J. Toly, P. L. McCarney, and K. Segbers, eds. 2011. *Cities and Global Governance.* Farnham: Ashgate.

Amiri, S., and E. Sevin, eds. 2020. *City Diplomacy: Current Trends and Future Prospects.* London: Palgrave.

Andranovich, G., M. J. Burbank, and C. H. Heying. 2001. "Olympic Cities: Lessons

Learned from Mega-Event Politics." *Journal of Urban Affairs* 23(2), 113–31. https://doi.org/10.1111/0735-2166.00079

Anheier, H., and H. Katz. 2005. "Network Approach to Global Civil Society." In H. Anheier, M. Glasius, and M. Kaldor (eds.), *Global Civil Society Yearbook 2004/5*, 206–21. London: Sage.

Ashworth, G. J. 1991. *War and the City*. London: Routledge.

Avant, D. D., M. Finnemore, and S. K. Sell, eds. 2010. *Who Governs the Globe?* Cambridge: Cambridge University Press.

Bansard, J. S., P. H. Pattberg, and O. Widerberg. 2017. "Cities to the Rescue? Assessing the Performance of Transnational Municipal Networks in Global Climate Governance." *International Environmental Agreements: Politics, Law and Economics* 17(2), 229–46. https://doi.org/10.1007/s10784-016-9318-9

Barber, B. 2013. *If Mayors Ruled the World: Dysfunctional Nations, Rising Cities*. New Haven: Yale University Press.

Barber, S. 1997. "Strategic Alliances: International, Local and Regional Government Alliances." *Public Money and Management* 17(4), 19–23. https://doi.org/10.1111/1467-9302.00087

Bartels, L. M. 2010. *Unequal Democracy: The Political Economy of the New Gilded Age*. Princeton: Princeton University Press.

Baycan-Levent, T., A. A. Gülümser Akgün, and S. Kundak. 2010. "Success Conditions for Urban Networks: Eurocities and Sister Cities." *European Planning Studies* 18(8), 1187–206. https://doi.org/10.1080/09654311003791259

Beall, J., and D. Adam. 2017. *Cities, Prosperity and Influence. The Role of City Diplomacy in Shaping Soft Power in the 21st Century*. London: British Council.

Beauregard, R. A., and J. Pierre. 2000. "Disputing the Global: A Sceptical View of Locality-Based International Initiatives." *Policy and Politics* 28(4), 465–78. https://doi.org/10.1332/0305573002501081

Beaverstock, J. V., R. G. Smith, and P. J. Taylor. 2000. "World-City Network: A New Metageography?" *Annals of the Association of American Geographers* 90(1), 123–34. https://doi.org/10.1111/0004-5608.00188

Belfanti, C. M. 2019. *Storia culturale del Made in Italy*. Bologna: Il Mulino.

Bendel, P., and J. Stürner. 2019. "The Two-Way 'Glocalisation' of Human Rights or How Cities Become International Agents in Migration Governance." *Peace, Human Rights, Governance* 3(2), 215–40.

Betsill, M. M. 2006. "Transnational Actors in International Environmental Politics." In M. M. Betsill, K. Hochstetler, and D. Stevis (eds.), *Palgrave Advances in International Environmental Politics*, 172–202. Basingstoke: Palgrave.

Betsill, M. M., and H. Bulkeley. 2004. "Transnational Networks and Global Environmental Governance: The Cities for Climate Protection Program." *International Studies Quarterly* 48(2), 471–93.

Björkdahl, A. 2013. "Urban Peacebuilding." *Peacebuilding* 1(2), 207–21. https://doi.org/10.1080/21647259.2013.783254

Blank, Y. 2006. "The City and the World." *Columbia Journal of Transnational Law* 44(3), 868–931.

Bontenbal, M., and P. van Lindert. 2006. "Decentralized International Cooperation: North-South Municipal Partnerships." In P. van Lindert, A. de Jong, G. Nijenhuis, and G. van Westen (eds.), *Development Matters: Geographical Studies on Develop-*

ment Processes and Policies, 301–14. Utrecht: Utrecht University, Faculty of Geosciences.

Borja, J., and M. Castells. 1997. *Local and Global: The Management of Cities in the Information Age*. London: Earthscan.

Bouteligier, S. 2012. *Cities, Networks, and Global Environmental Governance: Space of Innovation, Place of Leadership*. London: Routledge.

Brookings Institution. 2018. *Global Metro Monitor 2018*. Retrieved from https://www.brookings.edu/research/global-metro-monitor-2018/

Bulkeley, H., and H. Schroeder. 2009. "Global Cities and the Governance of Climate Change: What Is the Role of Law in Cities?" *Fordham Urban Law Journal* 26(2), 313–59.

Busby, J. W. 2007. "Bono Made Jesse Helms Cry: Jubilee 200, Debt Relief, and Moral Action in International Politics." *International Studies Quarterly* 51(2), 247–75.

Bush, G. W. 2002. *The National Security Strategy of the United States of America*. September 17. Available at http://nssarchive.us/national-security-strategy-2002/

C40 Cities. 2020. *Global Mayors Launch COVID-19 Economic Recovery Taskforce*. Retrieved from https://www.c40.org/press_releases/global-mayors-covid-19-recovery-task-force

Cabral, R., P. Engelke, K. Brown, and A. Terman Wedner. 2014. "Diplomacy for a Diffuse World." Issue Brief, September, Atlantic Council, Washington, DC. http://www.atlanticcouncil.org/publications/issue-briefs/diplomacy-for-a-diffuse-world

Caponio, T. 2018. "Immigrant Integration Beyond National Policies? Italian Cities' Participation in European City Networks." *Journal of Ethnic and Migration Studies* 44(12), 2053–69. https://doi.org/10.1080/1369183X.2017.1341711

Caporaso, J. 1993. "International Relations Theory and Multilateralism: The Search for Foundations." In J. G. Ruggie (ed.), *Multilateralism Matters: The Theory and Praxis of an Institutional Form*, 51–90. New York: Columbia University Press.

Castán Broto, V. 2017. "Urban Governance and the Politics of Climate Change." *World Development* 93, 1–15. https://doi.org/10.1016/j.worlddev.2016.12.031

Castells, M. 1989. *The Rise of the Network Society*. Oxford: Blackwell.

Cerny, P. G. 2010. *Rethinking World Politics: A Theory of Transnational Neopluralism*. Oxford: Oxford University Press.

Chan, D. K.-h. 2016. "City Diplomacy and 'Glocal' Governance: Revitalizing Cosmopolitan Democracy." *Innovation: The European Journal of Social Science Research* 29(2), 134–60. https://doi.org/10.1080/13511610.2016.1157684

Cochrane, A., J. Peck, and A. Tickell. 1996. "Manchester Plays Games: Exploring the Local Politics of Globalization." *Urban Studies* 33(8), 1319–36.

Criekemans, D., ed. 2010. *Regional Sub-State Diplomacy Today*. Amsterdam: Brill Nijhoff.

Curtis, S. 2014. *The Power of Cities in International Relations*. London: Routledge.

Curtis, S. 2016. *Global Cities and Global Order*. Oxford: Oxford University Press.

Curtis, S., and M. Acuto. 2018. "The Foreign Policy of Cities." *The RUSI Journal* 163(6), 8–17. https://doi.org/10.1080/03071847.2018.1562014

Czempiel, E. O., and J. N. Rosenau. 1992. *Governance without Government: Order and Change in World Politics*. Cambridge: Cambridge University Press.

Davutoğlu, A. 2021. *Pivot Cities in the Rise and Fall of Civilizations*. London: Routledge.

della Porta, D., and S. Tarrow, eds. 2005. *Transnational Protest and Global Activism*. Lanham, MD: Rowman and Littlefield.

Department of Defense. 2012. *Sustaining US Global Leadership: Priorities for 21st Century Defense.* Washington, DC: Department of Defense.

Derudder, B., M. Hoyler, P. J. Taylor, and F. Witlox, eds. 2012. *International Handbook of Globalization and World Cities.* London: Edward Elgar.

Desch, M. 2001. *Soldiers in Cities: Military Operations on Urban Terrain.* Carlisle, PA: Strategic Studies Institute.

de Villiers, J. C. 2009. "Success Factors and the City-to-City Partnership Management Process—From Strategy to Alliance Capability." *Habitat International* 33(2), 149–56. https://doi.org/10.1016/j.habitatint.2008.10.018

Diani, M. 2003. "Networks and Social Movements: A Research Programme." In M. Diani and D. McAdam (eds.), *Social Movements and Networks: Relational Approaches to Collective Action*, 299–319. Oxford: Oxford University Press.

Dobbs, R., S. Smit, J. Remes, J. C. Manyika, C. Roxburgh, and A. Restrepo. 2011. *Urban World: Mapping the Economic Power of Cities.* New York: McKinsey Global Institute.

Duchacek, I. D., D. Latouche, and G. Stevenson. 1988. *Perforated Sovereignties and International Relations: Trans-Sovereign Contacts of Subnational Governments.* New York: Greenwood Press.

Ferguson, Y. H. 2015. "Diversity in IR Theory: Pluralism as an Opportunity for Understanding Global Politics." *International Studies Perspectives* 16(1), 3–12. https://doi.org/10.1111/insp.12092

Ferguson, Y. H., and R. W. Mansbach. 2008. *A World of Polities: Essays on Global Politics.* New York: Routledge.

Fisher, F. 1990. *Technocracy and the Politics of Expertise.* London: Sage.

Forcellese, T. 2013. *L'Italia e i Giochi Olimpici. Un secolo di candidature: politica, istituzioni e diplomazia sportiva.* Milan: Franco Angeli.

Friedmann, J. 1986. "The World City Hypothesis." *Development and Change* 17(1), 69–83. https://doi.org/10.1111/j.1467-7660.1986.tb00231.x

Friedmann, J., and G. Wolff. 1982. "World City Formation: An Agenda for Research and Action." *International Journal of Urban and Regional Research* 6(3), 309–44. https://doi.org/10.1111/j.1468-2427.1982.tb00384.x

Gartung, J. 2000. "Local Authorities as Peace Factors/Actors/Workers." *Journal of World-Systems Research* 6(3), 860–72. https://doi.org/10.5195/jwsr.2000.207

Giulianotti, R. 2015. "The Beijing 2008 Olympics: Examining the Interrelations of China, Globalization, and Soft Power." *European Review* 23(2), 286–96. https://doi.org/10.1017/S1062798714000684

Gottmann, J. 1989. "What Are Cities Becoming Centres Of? Sorting Out the Possibilities." In R. V. Knight and G. Gappert (eds.), *Cities in a Global Society.* Vol. 35. Newbury Park, CA: Sage.

Graham, S. 2010. *Cities Under Siege: The New Military Urbanism.* London: Verso.

Guidoni. 1992. *Le città dal medioevo al rinascimento.* Roma: Laterza.

Gutierrez-Camps, A. 2013. "Local Efforts and Global Impacts: A City-Diplomacy Initiative on Decentralisation." *Perspectives* 21(2), 49–61.

Haass, R. N. 2008. "The Age of Nonpolarity: What Will Follow U.S. Dominance?" *Foreign Affairs* 87(3), 44–56.

Habitat III. 2016. *The New Urban Agenda.* United Nations Conference on Housing ans

Sustainable Urban Development, 20 October. See https://habitat3.org/the-new-urb an-agenda/

Hachigian, N. 2019. "Cities Will Determine the Future of Diplomacy. Urban Centers Are Taking International Relations into Their Own Hands." *Foreign Policy* 4(16 April).

Hachigian, N., and A. F. Pipa. 2020. "Can Cities Fix a Post-Pandemic World Order?" *Foreign Policy* 5 (May 5).

Hafteck, P. 2003. "An Introduction to Decentralized Cooperation: Definitions, Origins and Conceptual Mapping." *Public Administration and Development* 23(4), 333–45. https://doi.org/10.1002/pad.286

Hale, T., and D. Held, eds. 2011. *Handbook of Transnational Governance: New Institutions and Innovations.* Cambridge: Polity.

Hall, R. B., and T. J. Biersteker, eds. 2002. *The Emergence of Private Authority in Global Governance.* New York: Cambridge University Press.

Hamilton, K., and R. Langhorne. 2011. *The Practice of Diplomacy. Its Evolution, Theory and Administration.* London: Routledge.

Held, D. 2002. "Law of People, Law of States." *Legal Theory* 8(1), 1–44.

Held, D., and A. McGrew, eds. 2002. *Governing Globalization: Power, Authority and Global Governance.* Cambridge: Polity.

Higgott, R. A., G. R. D. Underhill, and A. Bieler, eds. 2000. *Non-State Actors and Authority in the Global System.* New York: Routledge.

Hill, K. A., and J. E. Hughes. 1998. *Cyberpolitics: Citizen Activism in the Age of the Internet.* Lanham, MD: Rowman and Littlefield.

Hobbs, H. H. 1994. *City Hall Goes Abroad: The Foreign Policy of Local Politics.* Los Angeles: SAGE.

Hocking, B. 1993. *Localizing Foreign Policy: Non-Central Governments and Multilayered Diplomacy.* London: MacMillan.

Hocking, B., J. Melissen, S. Riordan, and P. Sharp. 2012. *Futures for Diplomacy: Integrative Diplomacy in the 21st Century.* Den Haag, Clingendael Netherlands Institute of International Relations.

Hoornweg, D., and K. Pope. 2014. *Socioeconomic Pathways and Regional Distribution of the World's 101 Largest Cities.* Toronto, Global Cities Institute Working Paper No. 04.

Hulme, D., and M. Edwards, eds. 1997. *NGOs, States and Donors: Too Close for Comfort?* London: Macmillan.

Huntington, S. P. 1993. "Clash of Civilizations?" *Foreign Affairs* 72(3), 22–49.

Huntington, S. P. 1996. *The Clash of Civilizations and the Remaking of World Order.* New York: Simon and Shuster.

Ikenberry, G. J. 2011. *Liberal Leviathan: The Origins, Crisis, and Transformation of the American World Order.* Princeton: Princeton University Press.

Jacobs, J. 1969. *The Economy of Cities.* New York: Random House.

Jayne, M., P. Hubbard, and D. Bell. 2011. "Worlding a City: Twinning and Urban Theory." *City* 15(1), 25–41. https://doi.org/10.1080/13604813.2010.511859

JLL Cities Research Center. 2015. *Globalisation and Competition: The New World of Cities.* Retrieved from http://www.jll.com/cities-research

Kagan, R. 1998. "The Benevolent Empire." *Foreign Policy* 111 (Summer), 24–35.

Kagan, R. 2012. *The World America Made*. New York: Knopf.

Kant, I. 1795; reprinted 1991. "Perpetual Peace: A Philosophical Sketch." In H. Reiss (ed.), *Kant's Political Writings*, 93–130. Cambridge: Cambridge University Press.

Kapoor, I. 2012. *Celebrity Humanitarianism: The Ideology of Global Charity*. London: Routledge.

Kavaratzis, M. 2004. "From City Marketing to City Branding: Towards a Theoretical Framework for Developing City Brands." *Place Branding* 1(1), 58–73. https://doi.org /10.1057/palgrave.pb.5990005

Kavaratzis, M., and G. J. Ashworth. 2005. "City Branding: An Effective Assertion of Identity or a Transitory Marketing Trick?" *Tijdschrift voor economische en sociale geografie* 96(5), 506–14. https://doi.org/10.1111/j.1467-9663.2005.00482.x

Keck, M., and K. Sikkink. 1998. *Activists Beyond Borders: Advocacy Networks in International Politics*. Ithaca: Cornell University Press.

Keohane, R. 1986. "Reciprocity in International Relations." *International Organization* 40(1), 1–27.

Keohane, R., and J. Nye. 1977. *Power and Interdependence*. Boston: Little, Brown.

Keohane, R., and J. Nye, eds. 1971. *Transnational Relations and World Politics*. Cambridge, MA: Harvard University Press.

Kern, K., and H. Bulkeley. 2009. "Cities, Europeanization and Multi-level Governance: Governing Climate Change through Transnational Municipal Networks." *JCMS: Journal of Common Market Studies* 47(2), 309–32. https://doi.org/10.1111/j.1468 -5965.2009.00806.x

Khanna, P. 2008. *The Second World: How Emerging Powers Are Redefining Global Competition in the XXI Century*. New York: Random House.

Khanna, P. 2011. *How to Run the World: Charting a Course to the Next Renaissance*. New York: Random House.

Khanna, P. 2016. *Connectography: Mapping the Future of Global Civilization*. New York: Random House.

Knox, P., and P. Taylor, eds. 1995. *World Cities in a World-System*. Cambridge: Cambridge University Press.

Koenig-Archibugi, M., and M. Zürn, eds. 2006. *New Modes of Governance in the Global System: Exploring Publicness, Delegation and Inclusiveness*. Basingstoke, UK: Palgrave Macmillan.

Kotler, P., D. H. Haider, and I. Rein. 1993. *Marketing of Places*. New York: Free Press.

Krasner, S. D. 1982. "Structural Changes and Regime Consequences: Regimes as Intervening Variables." *International Organization* 36(2), 185–205.

Krauthammer, C. 2003. "The Unipolar Moment Revisited." *The National Interest* 70, 5–17.

La Porte, T. 2013. "City Public Diplomacy in the European Union." In M. K. Davis Cross and J. Melissen (eds.), *European Public Diplomacy: Soft Power at Work*, 85–111. London: Palgrave.

Laguerre, M. S. 2019. *Global City-Twinning in the Digital Age*. Ann Arbor: University of Michigan Press.

Le Galès, P. 2002. *European Cities: Social Conflicts and Governance*. New York: Oxford University Press.

Lecours, A. 2002. "Paradiplomacy: Reflections on the Foreign Policy and International Relations of Regions." *International Negotiation* 7(1), 91–114.

Leffel, B. 2018. "Animus of the Underling: Theorizing City Diplomacy in a World Society." *The Hague Journal of Diplomacy* 13(4), 502–22. https://doi.org/10.1163/1871191X-13040025

Lipschutz, R. D. 1992. "Reconstructing World Politics: The Emergence of Global Civil Society." *Millennium: Journal of International Studies* 21(3), 389–420.

Ljungkvist, K. 2015. *The Global City 2.0: From Strategic Site to Global Actor.* New York: Routledge.

Lofland, J. 1993. *Polite Protesters: The American Peace Movement of the 1980s.* Syracuse, NY: Syracuse University Press.

Lucarelli, A., and P. O. Berg. 2011. "City Branding: A State-of-the-Art Review of the Research Domain." *Journal of Place Management and Development* 4(1), 9–27. https://doi.org/10.1108/17538331111117133

Lusk, K., and N. Gunkel. 2018. *Cities Joining Ranks: Policy Networks on the Rise.* Boston University Initiative on Cities. http://www.bu.edu/ioc/files/2018/04/Cities-Joining-Ranks-Final-Report.pdf

Marchetti, R. 2008. *Global Democracy: For and Against. Ethical Theory, Institutional Design, and Social Struggles.* London: Routledge.

Marchetti, R. 2016. *Global Strategic Engagement. States and Non-State Actors in Global Governance.* Lanham, MD: Lexington Books.

Marchetti, R., and M. Pianta. 2012. "Global Networks of Civil Society and the Politics of Change." In A. Ellersiek, M. Pianta, and P. Utting (eds.), *Global Justice Activism and Policy Reform in Europe: Understanding When Change Happens,* 93–111. London: Routledge.

Marchetti, R., and N. Tocci. 2009. "Conflict Society: Understanding the Role of Civil Society in Conflict." *Global Change, Peace and Security* 21(2), 201–17.

Massey, D. 2007. *World City.* London: Polity.

Mazzucchelli, M. 2011. *Pace e diritti umani nei Comuni, nelle Province e nelle Regioni. L'infrastruttura normative e istituzionale.* Padova: Cleup.

McAdam, D., J. D. McCarthy, and M. N. Zald. 1996. *Comparative Perspectives on Social Movements: Political Opportunities, Mobilizing Structures, and Cultural Framings.* Cambridge: Cambridge University Press.

McFarland, A. S. 2004. *Neopluralism: The Evolution of the Political Process Theory.* Lawrence: University of Kansas Press.

Musch, A., ed. 2008. *City Diplomacy: The Role of Local Governments in Conflict Prevention, Peace-Building, and Post-Conflict Reconstruction.* The Hague: VNG International.

Naìm, M. 2013. *The End of Power. From Boardrooms to Battlefields and Churches to States, Why Being in Charge Isn't What It Used to Be.* New York: Basic Books.

Nye, J., and R. O. Keohane. 1971. "Transnational Relations and World Politics." *International Organization* 25(3), 329–49; 721–48.

Obama, B. 2007. "Renewing American Leadership." *Foreign Affairs* 86(4), 2–16.

OECD. 2020. *Tackling Coronavirus (Covid-19), Contributing to a Global Effort, Cities Policy Responses.* Retrieved from http://www.oecd.org/coronavirus/policyresponses/cities-policy-responsesfd1053ff/

Olesen, T. 2005. *International Zapatismo: The Construction of Solidarity in the Age of Globalization.* London: Zed Books.

Oomen, B., M. F. Davis, and M. Grigolo, eds. 2016. *Global Urban Justice: The Rise of Human Rights Cities.* New York: Cambridge University Press.

Oosterlynck, S., L. Beeckmans, D. Bassens, B. Derudder, B. Segaert, and L. Braeckmans, eds. 2018. *The City as a Global Political Actor.* London: Routledge.

Pianta, M., A. Ellersiek, and P. Utting. 2012. "How Can Activism Make Change Happen?" In P. Utting, M. Pianta, and A. Ellersiek (eds.), *Global Justice Activism and Policy Reform in Europe,* 297–322. London: Routledge.

Powell, W. M. 1990. "Neither Market nor Hierarchy; Network Forms of Organization." *Research in Organizational Behavior* 12, 295–336.

Price, M., and L. Benton-Short. 2008. *Migrants to the Metropolis: The Rise of Immigrant Gateway Cities.* Syracuse, NY: Syracuse University Press.

Prichard, A. 2017. "Collective Intentionality, Complex Pluralism and the Problem of Anarchy." *Journal of International Political Theory* 13(3), 360–77. https://doi.org/10.1177/1755088217715789

Putnam, R. D. 1988. "Diplomacy and Domestic Politics: The Logic of Two-Level Games." *International Organization* 42, 427–60.

Reckien, D., M. Salvia, O. Heidrich, J. M. Church, Pietrapertosa, S. De Gregorio-Hurtado . . . R. Dawson. 2018. "How Are Cities Planning to Respond to Climate Change? Assessment of Local Climate Plans from 885 Cities in the EU-28." *Journal of Cleaner Production* 191, 207–19. https://doi.org/10.1016/j.jclepro.2018.03.220

Risse-Kappen, T. 1994. "Ideas Do Not Float Freely: Transnational Coalitions, Domestic Structures, and the End of the Cold War." *International Organization* 48, 185–214.

Risse-Kappen, T., ed. 1995. *Bringing Transnational Relations Back In: Non-State Actors, Domestic Structure and International Institutions.* Ithaca: Cornell University Press.

Risse, T. 2011. *Governance Without a State? Policies and Politics in Areas of Limited Statehood.* New York: Columbia University Press.

Rodrigues, T., F. Brancoli, and P. Amar. 2017. "Global Cities, Global (in)Securities: An Introduction." *Contexto Internacional* 39, 467–76.

Rosenau, J. N. 1992. "Citizenship in a Changing Global Order." In J. N. Rosenau and E. O. Czempiel (eds.), *Governance without Government: Order and Change in World Politics,* 272–94. Cambridge: Cambridge University Press.

Rosenau, J. N. 1997. *Along the Domestic-Foreign Frontier: Exploring Governance in a Turbulent World.* Cambridge: Cambridge University Press.

Routledge, P. 2010. "Introduction: Cities, Justice and Conflict." *Urban Studies* 47(6), 1165–77. https://doi.org/10.1177/0042098009360240

Rudakowska, A., and C. Simon, 2020. "International City Cooperation in the Fight Against Covid-19: Behind the Scenes Security Providers." *Global Policy* (September), 1–14.

Ruggie, J. G. 1982. "International Regimes, Transactions, and Change: Embedded Liberalism in the Postwar Economic Order." *International Organization* 36(2), 379–415.

Ruggie, J. G. 1993. "Multilateralism: The Anatomy of an Institution." In J. G. Ruggie (ed.), *Multilateralism Matters: The Theory and Praxis of an Institutional Form,* 3–47. New York: Columbia University Press.

Sassen, S. 2000. *Cities in a World Economy.* 2nd ed. Thousand Oaks, CA: Pine Forge Press.

Sassen, S. 2001. *The Global City: New York, London, Tokyo.* 2nd ed. Princeton: Princeton University Press.

Sassen, S. 2002. "Global Cities and Diasporic Networks: Microsites in Global Civil

Society." In M. Glasius, M. Kaldor, and H. Anheier (eds.), *Global Civil Society 2002*, 217–38. Oxford: Oxford University Press.

Sassen, S. 2004. "Local Actors in Global Politics." *Current Sociology* 52, 649–70.

Sassen, S. 2014. *Expulsions: Brutality and Complexity in the Global Economy*. Cambridge, MA: Harvard University Press.

Scholte, J. A. 2004. "Civil Society and Democratically Accountable Global Governance." *Government and Opposition* 39(2), 211–33.

Schulz, M. S. 1998. "Collective Action across Borders: Opportunity Structures, Network Capacities, and Communicative Praxis in the Age of Advanced Globalization." *Sociological Perspectives* 41(3), 587–616.

Setzer, J. 2015. "Testing the Boundaries of Subnational Diplomacy: The International Climate Action of Local and Regional Governments." *Transnational Environmental Law* 4(2), 319–37.

Sharp, P. 2003. "Making Sense of Citizen Diplomats: The People of Duluth, Minnesota, as International Actors." *International Studies Perspectives* 2(2), 131–50. https://doi.org/10.1111/1528-3577.00045

Shoval, N. 2002. "A New Phase in the Competition for the Olympic Gold: The London and New York Bids for the 2012 Games." *Journal of Urban Affairs* 24(5), 583–99. https://doi.org/10.1111/1467-9906.00146

Shuman, M. H. 1986. "Dateline Main Street: Local Foreign Policies." *Foreign Policy* 65, 154–74. https://doi.org/10.2307/1148845

Shuman, M. H. 1992. "Dateline Main Street: Courts v. Local Foreign Policies." *Foreign Policy* 86, 158–77. https://doi.org/10.2307/1149195

Slaughter, A.-M. 2003. "A Global Community of Courts." *Harvard International Law Journal* 44, 191–220.

Slaughter, A.-M. 2004. *A New World Order*. Princeton: Princeton University Press.

Smith, J. 2017. "Responding to Globalization and Urban Conflict: Human Rights City Initiatives." *Studies in Social Justice* 11(2).

Smith, J., and D. Wiest. 2012. *Social Movements in the World-System: The Politics of Crisis and Transformation*. New York: Russell Sage Foundation.

Smith, N. P. 1988. "Paradiplomacy between the U.S. and Canadian Provinces: The Case of Acid Rain Memoranda of Understanding." *Journal of Borderlands Studies* 3(1), 13–38. https://doi.org/10.1080/08865655.1988.9695350

Soldatos, P. 1990. "An Explanatory Framework for the Study of Federal States as Foreign-Policy Actors." In H. J. Michelman and P. Soldatos (eds.), *Federalism and International Relations: The Role of Subnational Units*, 34–53. Oxford: Clarendon Press.

Stanley, B. 2003. "City Wars or Cities of Peace: (Re)Integrating the Urban into Conflict Resolution." *GaWC Research Bulletin*, 123.

Stanley, B. 2005. "Middle East City Networks and the 'New Urbanism.'" *Cities* 22(3), 189–99. https://doi.org/10.1016/j.cities.2005.03.007

Stren, R., and A. Friendly. 2019. "Toronto and São Paulo: Cities and International Diplomacy." *Urban Affairs Review* 55(2), 375–404. https://doi.org/10.1177/1078087417722862

Tarrow, S. 2005. *The New Transnational Activism*. Cambridge: Cambridge University Press.

Tavares, R. 2016. *Paradiplomacy: Cities and States as Global Players*. New York: Oxford University Press.

Taylor, P. J. 2004. *World City Network: A Global Urban Analysis.* London: Routledge.

Taylor, P. J. 2012a. "Historical City Networks." In B. Derudder (ed.), *International Handbook of Globalization and World Cities*, 9–21. London: Edward Elgar.

Taylor, P. J. 2012b. "On City Cooperation and City Competition." In B. Derudder, M. Hoyler, P. J. Taylor, and F. Witlox (eds.), *International Handbook of Globalization and World Cities*, 64–72. London: Edward Elgar.

Taylor, P. J. 2014. "A Research Odyssey: From Interlocking Network Model to Extraordinary Cities." *Tijdschrift voor economische en sociale geografie* 105(4), 387–97. https://doi.org/10.1111/tesg.12096

Taylor, P. J., P. Ni, B. Derudder, M. Hoyler, J. Huang, F. Lu, . . . W. Shen. 2009. "Measuring the World City Network: New Results and Developments." *GaWC Research Bulletin*, 300.

Ted Hewitt, W. E. 1999. "Cities Working Together to Improve Urban Services in Developing Areas: The Toronto–São Paulo Example." *Studies in Comparative International Development* 34(1), 27–44. https://doi.org/10.1007/BF02687603

Terruso, F. 2016. "Complementing Traditional Diplomacy: Regional and Local Authorities Going International." *European View* 15(2), 325–34. https://doi.org/10.1007/s12290-016-0405-7

Tuirán Sarmiento, Á. A., ed. 2016. *Acción internacional de los gobiernos locales o nuevas formas de diplomacia. Una mirada a la experiencia latinoamericana.* Barranquilla: Editorial Universidad del Norte.

United Cities and Local Governments. 2008. *The Hague Agenda on City Diplomacy.* The Hague, First World Conference on City Diplomacy, "The Role of Local Governments in Conflict Prevention, Peace-building and Post-Conflict Reconstruction."

United Nations. 2018. *The World's Cities in 2018.* New York: United Nations, Department of Economic and Social Affairs, Population Division. Data Booklet (ST/ESA/SER.A/417).

United Nations. 2019. *World Urbanization Prospects: The 2018 Revision.* New York: United Nations, Department of Economic and Social Affairs, Population Division (ST/ESA/SER.A/420).

United Nations Human Settlements Programme. 2011. *The Economic Role of Cities.* New York: United Nations, UN-HABITAT.

Valdani, E., and F. Ancarani. 2000. *Strategie di marketing del territorio.* Milan: Egea.

Van Der Pluijm, R., and J. Melissen. 2007. *City Diplomacy: The Expanding Role of Cities in International Politics.* Den Haag, Clingendael Netherlands Institute of International Relations.

van Overbeek, F. 2007. *City Diplomacy: The Roles and Challenges of the Peace Building Equivalent of Decentralized Cooperation.* Working Paper, University of Utrecht. http://www.peacepalacelibrary.nl/ebooks/files/371219574.pdf

Van Rooy, A. 2004. *The Global Legitimacy Game: Civil Society, Globalization, and Protest.* Houndmills, Basingstoke: Palgrave.

Viltard, Y. 2010. "Diplomatie des villes: collectivités territoriales et relations internationales." *Politique étrangère* 3, 593–604.

Warkentin, C. 2001. *Reshaping World Politics: NGOs, the Internet and Global Civil Society.* Lanham, MD: Rowman and Littlefield.

Weiss, T. G., and R. Wilkinson. 2019. *Rethinking Global Governance.* Cambridge: Polity.

Wiseman, G. 1999. *"Polylateralism" and New Modes of Global Dialogue.* London: Sage.

Woods, N. 2000. "Globalization and International Institutions." In N. Woods (ed.), *The Political Economy of Globalization*, 202–23. New York: St. Martin's Press.

World Bank. 2019. *Urban Development Data*. Washington, DC: World Bank.

Zheng, Y. N. 1994. "Perforated Sovereignty: Provincial Dynamism and China's Foreign Trade." *The Pacific Review* 7(3), 309–21. https://doi.org/10.1080/0951274940871 9100

Zürn, M. 2004. "Global Governance and Legitimacy Problems." *Government and Opposition* 39(2), 260–87.

Zürn, M. 2018. *A Theory of Global Governance: Authority, Legitimacy, and Contestation*. Oxford: Oxford University Press.

Index